The 1960-1969 CORVAIR

AUTHENTICITY SERIES

WAYNE MACHAN &
BILL BRUGGEN

ISBN 0-929758-07-2
Library of Congress Catalog Card Number: 89-063378

Published by Beeman Jorgensen, Inc.
7510 Allisonville Road, Suite 119, Indianapolis, IN 46250 U.S.A.

Printed and bound in the United States of America
Cover design and photography by Llew Kinst, Cupertino, California

First Printing, August 1991

Contents

To our wives, Mary Ellen and Rosemary, who
didn't say "NO!" to our newest scheme to put
a little mark on this great big world.

Acknowledgements

Joint authorship is an unusual venture. It requires a full load of sharing and compromise. The fact that we survived the ordeal of writing this book testifies to our saintly natures or a very deep friendship. We suspect the latter.

Reportedly, one of the most over used words in the english language is "I". We can proudly boast that " I" will not be found in this book. We expect to share the little fame the book may bring as well as the suffering from the inevitable mistakes, glitches and oversights.

In all honesty, this project was started with only the faintest knowledge of Corvairs. Bill owned a 1960 500 coupe almost 23 years ago, and Wayne is proficent at changing oil and wiper blades on most makes of cars. Obviously someone else had to help.

This book never would have been written without the help of Dr. Brett Johnson. He set out the ground rules, gave us an outline, and assured us it would be published. He also lied! He said it would be easy.

It is highly unlikely that the book would have been written without the help of the Circle City Corvair Club. Not a single member refused to answer our questions or failed to help when asked. We met many wonderful Corvair owners, but none more gracious than these club members. More about them later. We would like to especially acknowledge the help of Jean Allan. Her library of Corvair material is unsurpassed in the midwest. Her willingness to share it completely with two unknown writers was unbelievable.

We never set out to discover new and exciting things about the Corvair automobile. Our job was to read all the available literature, talk to Corvair owners, and study as many Corvairs as possible. With this background we hoped to produce a book, with plenty of pictures, that detailed the hundreds of changes to the Corvair passenger car in 10 years of production. We are indebted to the experts and fans of the Corvair. They have kept the car alive long after General Motors laid it to rest. We tried to confirm each fact from at least two sources and document it in pictures. Larry Claypool's "Stock Is" column was invaluable in the validation process. The writings of Mike Ellis, Tony Fiore, and others, were constantly spread around our work room.

Our technical panel consisted of Dan Brizendine, Bill Oates, and George Sears. Credit for the technical expertise of the book belongs to these selfless gentlemen.

The following individuals deserve special recognition for giving of their time, personal knowledge, access to literature and files and allowing us to examine their automobiles. Many Corvairs were photographed at the "Nationals" in Kansas City, on the streets, in backyards and junkyards, and the owners went unrecorded. To all those we owe an apologetic "thank you".

Jean Allan, Indianapolis, Indiana
Jim Coughlin, Brownsburg, Indiana
Phillip Haper, Lafayette, Indiana
Greg Means, Greenwood, Indiana
Roy Muradito, Plattsmouth, Nebraska
Phillip Riddle, Brownsburg, Indiana
Fred Rohr, Brownsburg, Indiana

Dan Brizendine, Greenwood, Indiana
Rick Fulkerson, Muncie, Indiana
John McCardle, Indianapolis, Indiana
C.E. Miller, Peoria, Illinois
Bill Oates, Mooresville, Indiana
Tom Robinson, Kenosha, Wisconsin
George Sears, Anderson, Indiana

Introduction

This book will examine the non-mechanical aspects of the standard production versions of the Chevrolet Corvair passenger car. The purpose of the text is to aid those enthusiasts who have taken the restoration challenge as well as to entertain the Corvair trivia buff. While there are bound to be some inaccuracies and uncertainties, we have attempted to put together a complete and accurate description of the various models of the Corvair. Our hope is that those who spot mistakes will step forward and share their information so that subsequent editions can be more accurate.

We had to draw the line somewhere, so we decided to ignore the truck models. We felt it would take another book to adequately cover those vehicles.

This is one of the "Authenticity Series" published by Beeman Jorgensen, and the first covering an American car. Beeman Jorgensen is noted for books on the Porsche and it is appropriate that the first American car should be the Corvair. Most Corvair fanatics know that the early prototype Corvairs were hidden in Porsche body shells. Engineers could test the engines, drive trains, and suspension under normal driving conditions without letting the cat out of the bag.

There is another coincidental tie between the Corvair and the Porsche. Karl Ludvigsen, who headed up the public relations team for the Corvair at General Motors, has written one of the best books on the Porsche entitled *Porsche, Excellence Was Expected.* So it is altogether fitting and proper that Beeman Jorgensen should make this their first American car effort.

The lasting quality of the Corvair attests to its greatness. As late as 1985 there were still about 18% of all Corvairs ever built still registered. This totals about 300,000 units still operating and is an unbelievable number still on the road almost 20 years after the last car rolled off the assembly line.

Jean's Machine

CHAPTER 1

The Models

When General Motors planned the introduction of the Corvair to the American car market, they aimed to do it in grand style. In fact, however, actual model production began rather slowly behind a major barrage of publicity.

Only two models, the standard 500 and the deluxe version 700, were available as four door sedans in October 1959. The two door Club Coupes in the standard and 700 series were added in January 1960 and in May the Corvair Monza 900 Club Coupe made an appearance. The five models had a combined sales of about 250,000 cars and the Corvair 700 four door sedan accounted for more than half of the sales. The Monza model was an instant success and only its late entry in the market prevented it from being the best seller. Although the Corvair did fairly well in 1960, the total sales were below Chevrolet's expectations.

The popularity of the Monza and the upscale 700 series was not lost on the brass at General Motors and they immediately changed the focus of the Corvair from an economy car to a sports car. The change was not evident in the showrooms until 1962. It takes at least one year for ideas to become reality in Detroit, where time is measured by production years rather than the Julian calendar.

In the interim, the number of 1961 models more than doubled as a four door station wagon, Corvan, Rampside pickup, and the Greenbrier van became available. The Lakewood station wagons, like the sedans and coupes, were offered in standard and deluxe versions. The Monza also became available in sedan form in 1961. Total production climbed to almost 290,000 cars and over 47,000 trucks.

Although the basic body style and number of models remained unchanged in 1962, General Motor's executives were substituting models like baseball coaches switching hitting lineups. The sedan, station wagon, and convertible were added to the Monza line. The 500 station wagon and sedan were retired. The Spyder option made its debut and total Corvair car sales reached 300,000. The innovative truck line peaked at just under 36,000 units.

By then the Corvair sports car image had caught on in the showrooms, and the small station wagons had little appeal in this new market. In 1963 only six Corvair automobile models were offered. They included the 500, 700, and Monza two door coupes; the 700, and Monza four door sedans; the Monza convertible; and three trucks, the Corvan, Rampside and Greenbrier. Total Corvair sales slumped to a little over 281,000 units.

In 1964 the Spyder was designated as two of the seven car models available. This sportster was offered in coupe and convertible styles. The coupe in the 700 series was dropped, but all other models offered in 1963 were again available in 1964. Unfortunately the car sales continued to slump and ended just under the 200,000 figure for this last year of the original design.

Although Ralph Nader and safety problems are widely credited for the poor sales figures, a more important reason was the appearance of the Ford Mustang. This hot new sports car, with a sticker price under the tired Corvair, was a bad omen for Chevrolet's proud innovative automobile.

The year of the big styling change, 1965, ushered in

a new model numbering system. The seven car models were represented by the 500, Monza and the Corsa series. The Monza outsold the other lines as sales climbed back to almost 250,000 cars.

No model changes were made in 1966 but the Greenbrier, the last of the truck line, was dropped. Sales fell to a new low of 109,000 cars as all but the diehard zealots admitted the end of the Corvair was near.

The Corsa model never saw production in 1967 and the three Monza and two 500 models only sold about 28,000 cars. Three models, the 500 coupe, Monza coupe, and Monza convertible totaled only slightly over 21,000 sales in the 1968 and abbreviated 1969 sales years.

Corvair Part Numbers

The parts numbering system for all Corvair models was kept simple and consistent through all production years. The system was easy to use and the number designations became very graphic after a little use.

The parts catalog put all replacement parts in a Prime Group number, Sub-Group category and finally an in- dividual part number. Within each group, parts were listed by model year, vehicle series, part number, number used per vehicle, right-hand and left-hand designations, part name, and a description. Table 1-1 details the designations.

More of Jean's Machines

TABLE 1-1 CORVAIR PART NUMBERS

GROUP	SUBGROUP	PART
0.000 Engine - Clutch	0.423	Head Gasket
1.000 Coolant - Grille - Oil Systems	1.064	Blower Assembly
2.000 Chassis - Electrical Systems	2.275	Generator Assembly
3.000 Fuel - Exhaust - Carburetion	3.734	Carburetor Bowl
4.000 Transmission - Brakes	4.103	Transmission Case
5.000 Brakes - Rear Axle and Drive	5.809	Drum Assembly
6.000 Front Axle - Steering	6.897	Bushing Assembly
7.000 Frame - Springs - Bumper	7.831	Front Bumper
8.000 Sheet Metal - Heater	8.845	Heater
9.000 Body Mounting - Air Conditioning	9.260	Side outlet A/C Hose
10.000 Windshield - Doors - Controls	10.351	Door Assembly
11.000 Rear Glass - Seat and Adjuster	11.011	Glass Quarter Window
12.000 Metal Trim and Clips - Panels	12.800	Grille, Cowl Top
13.000 Body Wiring - Folding Top Trim (Group 13.000 has only a few convertible items)	13.095	Circuit Breaker
14.000 Folding Top Parts - Interior Trim	14.688	Door Arm Rest
15.000 Rear Trim - Mats - Yardage	15.530	Fabric Top & Wall Lining
16.000 Interior and Panels (Truck Interior and Panels)		
17.000 Single and Double Unit Body Parts (All Truck Body Parts)		

MODEL NUMBERING SYSTEM

The white collar staff that was responsible for developing an understandable, usable organizational system to help keep track of the Corvair did a very commendable job.

Beginning in 1960, the basic, standard automobile was designated as the 500 series. All cars in that family carried a numerical designation that started with 5. Deluxe models began with a 7 number, and the Monza or sport model started with a 9. The 1962 and 1963 Spyders were Monza options so they carried the 9 designation. In 1964 the Spyder became a separate model and was designated with a 6 as the first digit of the numerical code.

Two door models were coded "27", while the short lived station wagons carried "35" and convertible models were distinguished with a "67". The system was rounded off with the four door designation of "69".

This made the number designations for the various models quite easy to understand. A four door basic Corvair was designated as 569. A deluxe model two door was numbered as 727. A Monza two door model number was 927 and a Spyder convertible was a 667.

The system was easy to expand. __If__ the brass at Chevrolet had decided they wanted a basic convertible (567), or a Spyder station wagon (635), the numbering system would have accommodated the decision. Of course there were no basic convertibles or Spyder wagons built.

The second generation Corvairs carried a different numbering system, but it was just as sensible. The basic models were numbered 101. Despite the change in numbers, however, the basic model continued to be called the "500". The Monza was designated as 105, and the Corsa numbers began with 107.

The two door designation became "37", the four door number "39", and the convertible remained a "67". Therefore a Monza four door was a 10539, and a Corsa convertible was 10767.

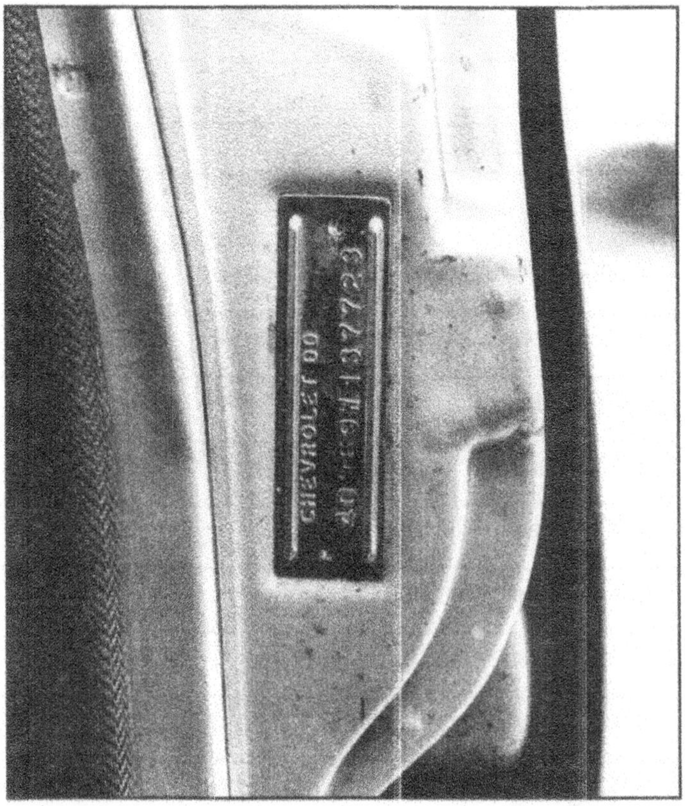

Look for the serial number plate on the left side lock post or center pillar on early models.

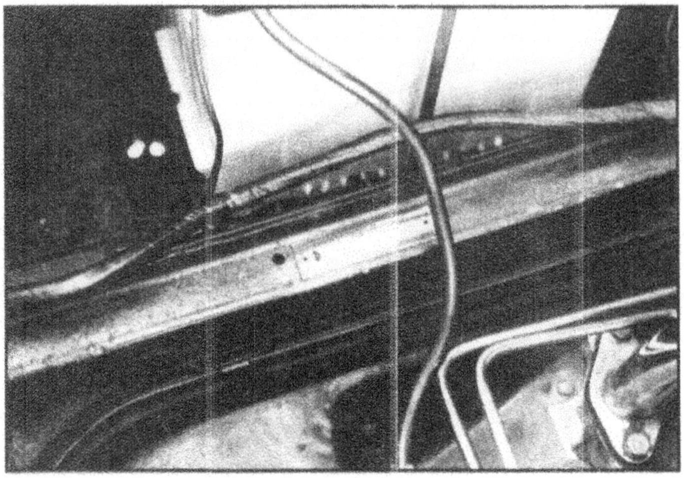

Beginning in 1965 the serial number plate was moved to the frame rail in the engine compartment. close to the battery.

COMPONENT NUMBERING SYSTEMS AND LOCATIONS

The numbering on the identification plates described the Corvair. On the early two door models the serial number plate was located on the left side lock post. For the four door models, it was located on the center pillar on the left side.

The last change, in 1967, was mandated by D.O.T. The serial number plate was moved to the top corner of the dash on the driver's side.

The Corvair was assembled at several plants across the country during its lifetime. WR or W denote Willow Run (Detroit); F, Flint, Michigan; O or OA, Oakland California; L or VN, Van Nuys, California; S- St Louis; and K or KC, Kansas City. In most cases the serial number had one letter, while the body plate used a multi-letter designation.

The Corvair was also assembled in Canada. The plant was located in Oshawa, Ontario, a medium sized town east of Toronto on the shore of Lake Ontario. Many of the knocked down Corvairs were made here and shipped overseas for assembly. Oshawa has a history of automaking and is now the home of the Canadian Auto Museum.

Late model body plates are located on the rear frame member.

The body plate was located on the rear frame member in the engine compartment. In addition to the same information that was found in the serial number, the body plate had the paint and trim numbers. This information is priceless to the restorer. A list of body paint and trim numbers can be found on page 93.

The first series of numbers in the serial number denoted the model number and year it was built. A letter, which designated the assembly plant, followed these numbers. One or two letters were followed by another series of numbers. This second series of numbers was the consecutive production number. For example: 5271W102436 described the car as a two door 500 model, built in 1961 at the Willow Run plant in Michigan. It was the 2,436th car off the assembly line that year.

The consecutive production number was somewhat misleading since **each plant** started numbering at 100,001 **each year!** Whether this was to impress the public with the number sold, or to reassure the car buyer early in the model year, or for some very logical reason, is unclear.

A Corvair with a serial number reading 107376L100567 has a pedigree as follows: Model 10737 (Monza convertible), built in 1966 at Los Angeles (actually the Van Nuys Plant) and it was the 567th car off the line that year. The 1969 models were the only ones that deviated from this system. That year the numbering scheme started with 700,001.

Now for a quiz. What are the details of a Corvair with a serial number reading 107679W700269? You got it! Model number 10767 (Corsa two door); built in 1969 at the Willow Run plant and it was the 269th car built that year. No, we have not gone completely nuts from too much proof reading. We know there are no actual cars with these serial numbers and we don't own the only Corsa built in 1969!!

1960 THROUGH 1964 MODEL DESIGNATIONS

MODEL	1960	1961	1962	1963	1964
Corvair Std. 2 door	527	527	527	527	527
Corvair Std. 4 Door	569	569	Not Offered	Not Offered	Not Offered
Deluxe 2 Door	727	727	727	727	Not Offered
Deluxe 4 Door	769	769	769	769	769
Lakewood Std. Station Wagon	Not Offered	535	Not Offered	Not Offered	Not Offered
Lakewood Deluxe Station Wagon	Not Offered	735	735	Not Offered	Not Offered
Monza 2 Door	927	927	927	927	927
Monza 4 Door	Not Offered	969	969	969	969
Monza Station Wagon	Not Offered	Not Offered	935	Not Offered	Not Offered
Monza Convertible	Not Offered	Not Offered	967	967	967
Spyder 2 Door	Not Offered	Not Offered	Not Offered	Offered as Monza	627
Spyder Convertible	Not Offered	Not Offered	Not Offered	Offered as Monza	667

1965 THROUGH 1969 MODEL DESIGNATIONS

MODEL	1965	1966	1967	1968 &1969
500 2 Door	10137	10137	10137	10137
500 4 Door	10139	10139	10139	Not Offered
Monza 2 Door	10537	10537	10537	10537
Monza 4 Door	10539	10539	10539	Not Offered
Monza Convertible	10567	10567	10567	10567
Corsa 2 Door	10737	10737	Not Offered	Not Offered
Corsa Convertible	10767	10767	Not Offered	Not Offered

John's machine

MODELS AND PRODUCTION YEARS

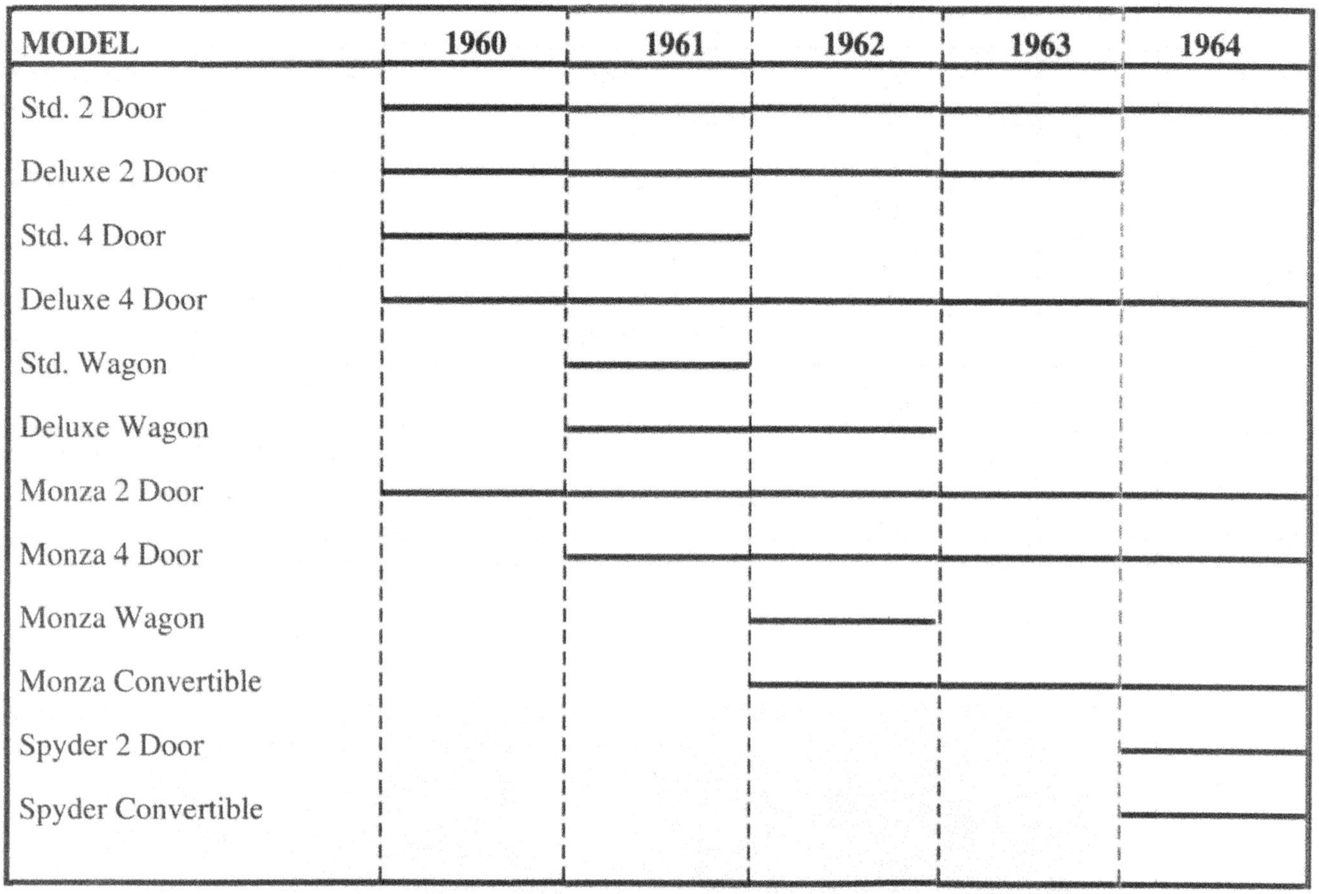

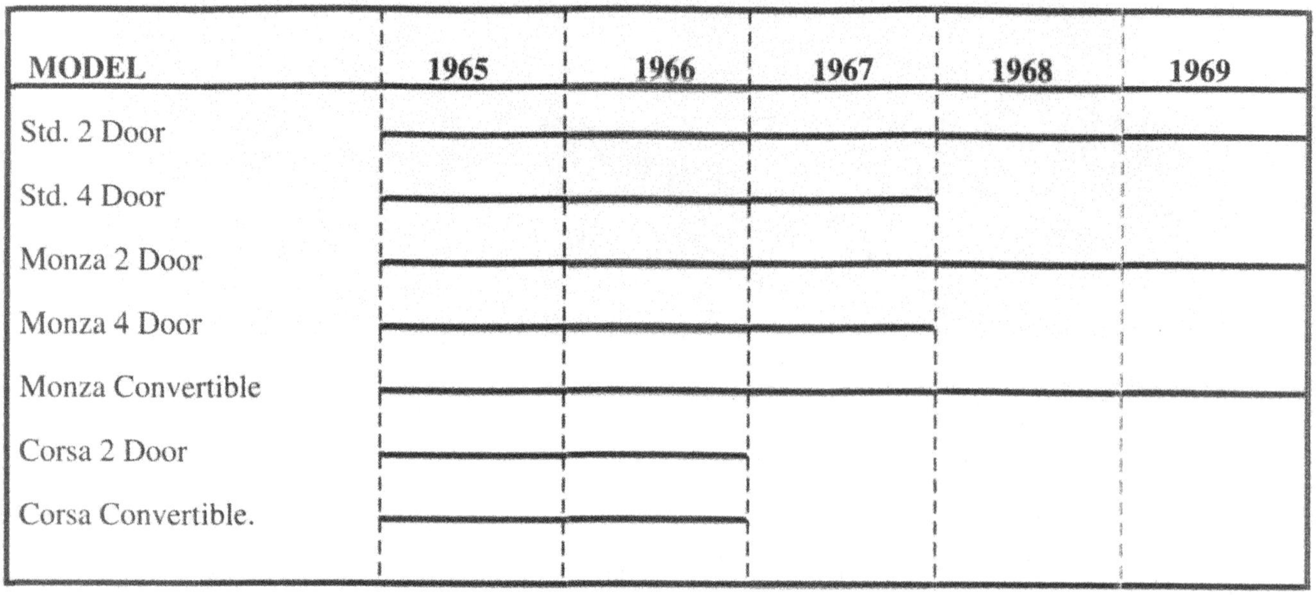

Chapter 2

Chassis

Unitized Construction

The Corvair was General Motors first attempt at producing a full line of cars with a completely unitized body. Instead of fastening sheet metal to a rigid frame, the Corvair featured individual units welded together to form a self-supporting box.

The floor and door sill were welded to form a single unit.

Many of the components had an inner and outer shell which increased the strength of the "box". The main structural members were square tube like structures located near the reinforced sill members. Extensions of these members extended into the front and rear sections of the body and were welded to the wheel houses. There were approximately 6,450 spot welds used to make the unitized body of the Corvair, according to information from Fisher Body.

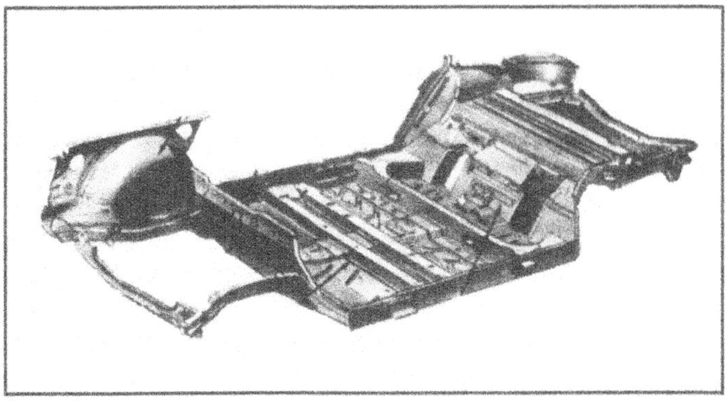

Illustration 12–20P 1976 Edition of the Chassis and Body Parts Catalog.

Although body repairmen shuddered at first, the new construction certainly put a lighter, more rigid, and stronger vehicle on the highway. The new construction allowed ample interior room while lowering the roof considerably. The almost dead flat floor was a noticeable improvement from the step ups and step downs of the time. The total weight of the vehicle was reduced, increasing fuel efficiency.

There were some drawbacks to the unitized construction however. Noise and vibration carried better through a unitized body. Sympathetic harmonic vibrations, or drumming, are generated throughout the welded unit. Insulation was used liberally in the Corvair to break up the resonance and block the noise.

Engine Compartment

While it is not the intention of this book to delve into the mechanical aspects of the Corvair, a few items are worth noting. The Corvair was the most successful rear engine American car. The Adams-Farwell, manufactured in Dubuque, Iowa, may have been the first.

The Julien, in the 1920's, and the Tucker, introduced after the Second World War, were others. All had rear engines, but were very short lived. The Adams-Farwell had a 108" wheelbase, exactly what the engineers at Chevrolet settled on after many experiments. They could have saved countless hours of work if they had just done their homework.

The Corvair engine was novel because it was air cooled. The advantages of a rear engine and air cooling were well documented. They included tremendous traction, incredible balance when braking, no bothersome "hump" in the floor, less weight than a water based cooling system, and less noise in the passenger compartment. Engine clatter was left in the wind wake of the car at highway speeds.

While the air cooled engine had advantages for the driver, it was a worry for the engineers. An oil cooler was needed to keep engine oil temperature at a tolerable level. The one used on 1960 through 1962 models looked like a mini radiator. A new design was introduced in 1962 and consisted of three plates. Spyders and air conditioned cars were equipped with a larger model containing eight cooling plates. High oil temperatures continued to be a problem. In 1964 the eight plate unit became standard and a twelve plate design was introduced for the Spyder models and cars equip- ped with air conditioning and 140 H.P. engines. The 1965 redesign efforts centered on supplying side covers to the larger oil coolers to retain air around the plates for additional cooling.

An interesting feature of the station wagon was that the oil level could be checked and oil added without disrupting a loaded cargo space. The oil filler pipe and dipstick could be reached through a hinged panel beneath the tail gate.

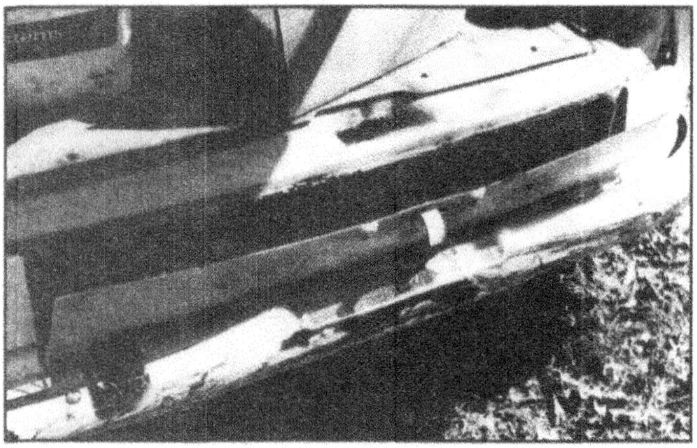

The station wagon had an engine service panel beneath the tail gate.

The long oil filler tube was easily accessible through the service panel.

The engine well included rear fender intrusions and the space was crammed with equipment. After 1960 the spare tire was added to the clutter.

The spare tire mounted in the engine compartment of this 1965 Monza illustrates the tight quarters.

The battery was another piece of equipment crammed into the engine compartment. In 1960 it was on the passenger side of the engine compartment. The battery was moved to the driver's side tucked behind the wheel well in 1961. When installed correctly, the positive terminal was toward the front of the car. The first generation cars used a group 53 battery. It was rated at 42 amp hours and contained nine plates per cell. The second generation Corvairs used a group 22F battery as standard equipment or a Group 24 heavy duty optional battery.

A plastic liner was added to the battery tray in mid 1963 to protect against corrosion. Although the liner size changed with different size batteries, the tray remained a feature until the end of production.

Battery gas in the engine compartment was a problem. The engine compartment was hot, especially in the summer or if the winter/summer door was not in proper position. Battery acid sometimes boiled over. In 1964 a venting system was devised. The individual battery caps were replaced with a molded cap that covered three of the filler holes. This cap was fitted with a small rubber hose (about the size of a straw) that diverted the gases and acid out of the engine compartment. Two cap units were needed for each battery, and the hoses were routed out the floor of the engine compartment.

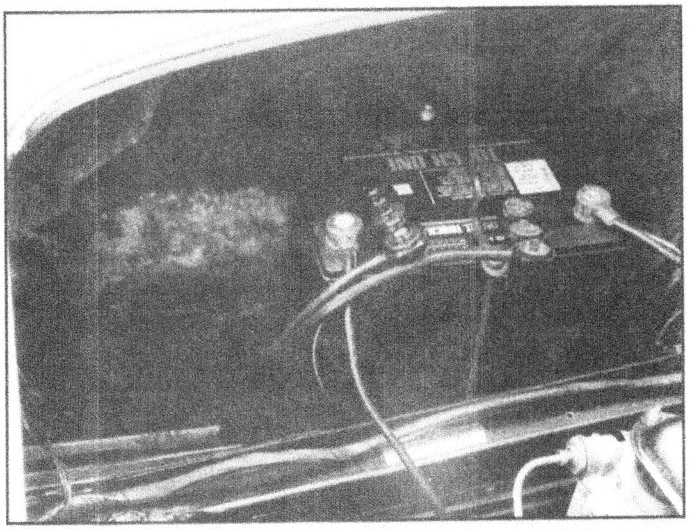

The battery gas venting system was improved by 1965.

The battery in the 1960 Corvair was held in place with a rubber covered metal retainer bar over the top. One end of the retainer was bolted to the fender and the other end was connected to a conventional hooked or "J" bolt that fastened to the battery tray. The 1961 hold down consisted of "J" bolts on both sides of the battery, fastened to the retainer bar. In 1963, a plastic strap replaced the metal retainer bar.

In 1965 the hold down system changed, returning to the rubber covered metal retainer bar and the single "J" bolt on the outboard side of the battery. The other end of the retainer was held in place by a long bolt that fastened to a nut welded to the fender wall.

In 1966 the battery hold down system was changed for the last time. A single hold down plate was tightened by one bolt. This wedge system forced the battery against a metal lip that held the battery.

A battery hold down wedge was used on all General Motors cars in 1966. Although this new system proved to be undesirable, it was continued on Corvair models until the end of production. The most serious flaw in the hold down wedge system was that it required a standard replacement battery. General Motors returned to the retainer bar and "J" bolt system too late to benefit Corvair.

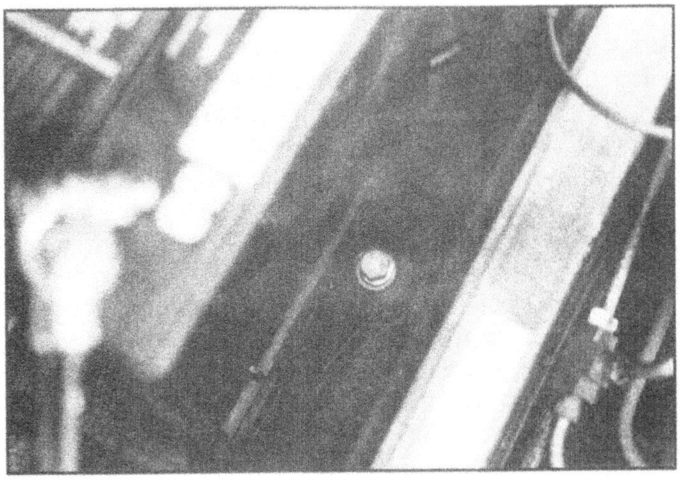

Although easy to use, the wedge battery hold down was not entirely successful.

The Corvair used a "spring ring" battery cable from Delco Remy as standard equipment. Although they were used on many General Motors cars, they were discontinued in the 1970's and are difficult to find today.

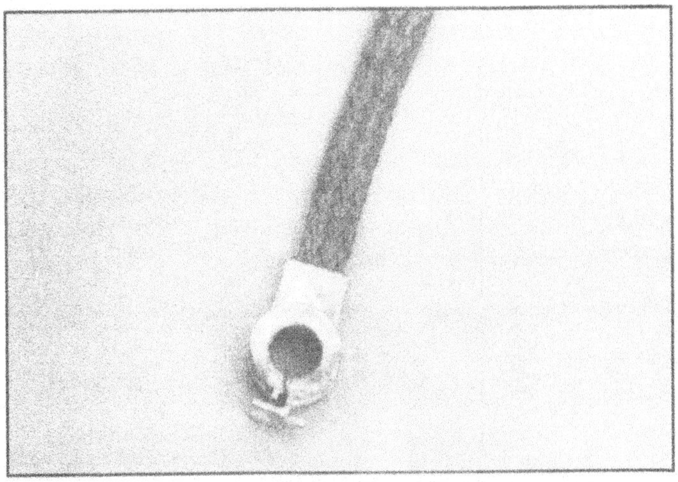

It appears the "spring ring" battery cable clamp was used on the Corvair throughout production.

The 1964 ground cable connected to a bumper brace bolt and to the generator mount.

The ground cable for the 1960 Corvair was fastened at the battery and to a bumper brace bolt. Another cable fastened at the bumper brace bolt and to the coil stud bolt on the cylinder head. From 1961 through 1964 the ground cable was a one piece strap that connected to a bumper brace bolt and to a bolt on the generator mount. A fusible link was added to the positive lead for the primary circuit in 1967.

According to Larry Claypool, the technical expert for CORSA, and certainly the most knowledgeable expert we came across, the paint used on the inside of the engine compartment for all 1960 through 1962 models was the exterior body color. The 1963 cars assembled in Oakland California continued to use the body paint, but sometime in mid–1963 the Willow Run Michigan plant changed from using body color to matte black.

Cars built outside the U.S. continued to use the body paint on the engine compartment. All cars built in the U.S. from 1964 through 1969 used black paint.

An insulation pad to muffle engine noise was installed between the engine compartment and the rear seat on the 1960 and 1961 models. The pad itself was felt and was covered with a black plastic film. It was about one inch thick.

In 1962 the panel behind the back seat of coupes was redesigned with a three layer pad to deaden the clatter from the engine compartment. The felt pad was continued on four door models.

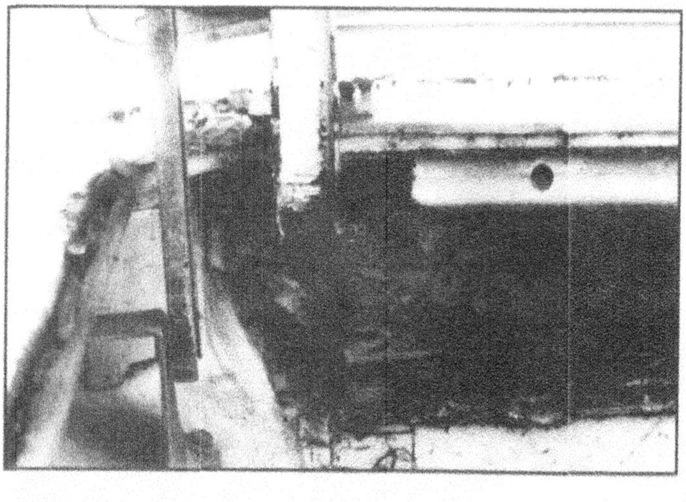

This insulation mat was installed on a 1961 700 model.

Second generation Monzas and Corsas carried insulation on the inside of the rear fenders, the rear quarter panels, and the wheel wells. The insulation was a thin fiberglass blanket.

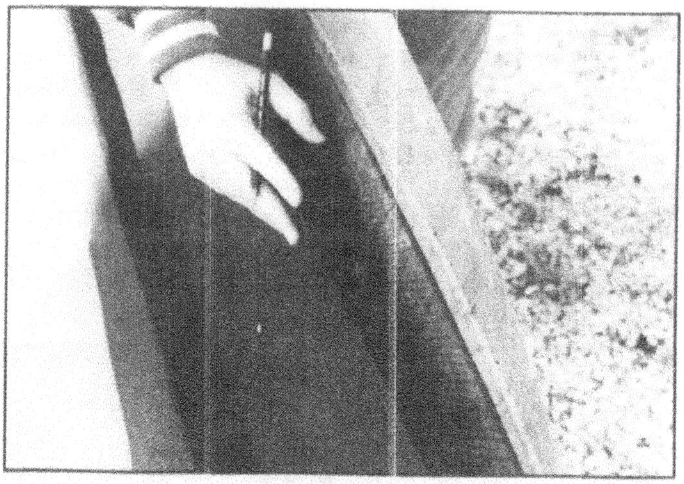

The three layer insulation pad shown in the photo was removed from a 1963 model.

The firewall was a solid piece of sheet metal in all 1960 through 1964 models. After 1965 when the engine air was drawn through the rear cowl grille, the wall between the engine compartment and passenger compartment was redesigned with openings in the sheet metal to permit free air flow.

Four openings in the second generation firewall provided air passage to the engine compartment.

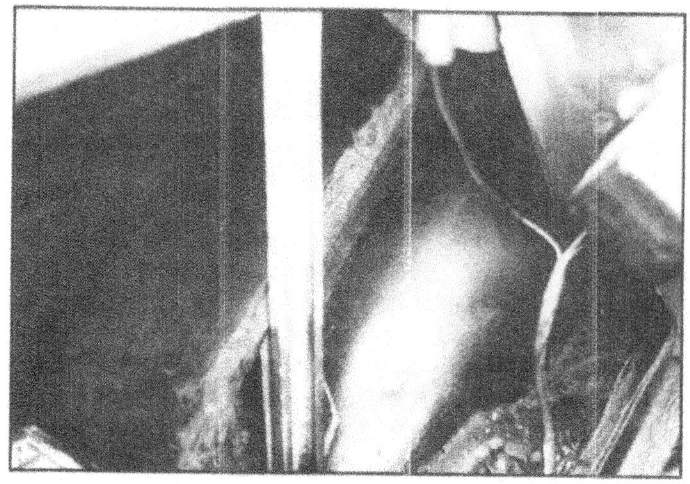

Wheel well pads were used in late models.

Luggage Compartment

The plan to build a rear engine car necessitated that the main luggage compartment be in the front. This was another first for the Corvair.

The luggage compartment was not overly large. The fact that luggage had to share the space with some items of equipment made the problem worse. The concave front panel on the 1960 models was another intrusion on a cramped luggage area.

The windshield washer bottle and holder, front headlight buckets and wiring, master cylinder filler cap, and later the master cylinder itself, wiper motor, gas heater (1960-1962), the spare tire (full size in those years), the jack and lug wrench all shared the trunk with personal baggage.

By 1961, the designers saw the error of their ways and made some important changes. The front of the luggage compartment was pushed out into a convex shape. The spare tire was moved to the engine compartment. The spare only returned to the luggage compartment if the car was equipped with air conditioning.

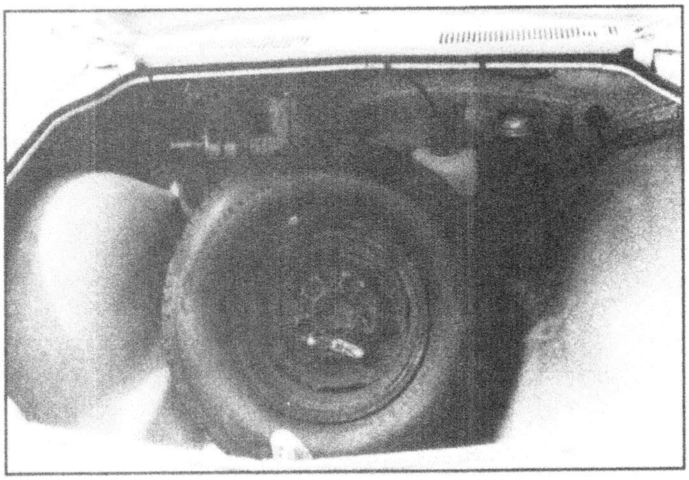

Air conditioning in this 1966 model relegated the spare tire to the luggage compartment.

The spare tire and tools returned to the luggage compartment with the 1969 convertibles equipped with the 140 engine. By that time, the designers did not have to woo future buyers and luggage space was a very minor consideration in a Corvair sale.

For the 1963 model year, the optional gasoline heater was discontinued. This change maximized the luggage compartment space for the first generation Corvairs.

Very little has been written on the subject of luggage compartment paint except for Larry Claypool's detailed account. Based on his observations, in 1960 the interior of the luggage space was painted the same color as the body. This practice continued on cars assembled in Canada, between 1961 and 1966. The inner panel of the front lid was painted the color of the body throughout the production of the Corvair.

Beginning in 1961, the paint color of the luggage compartment of all Corvairs assembled in the U.S. was changed to a white and gray spatter paint. Beginning in 1966, cars assembled in California used an

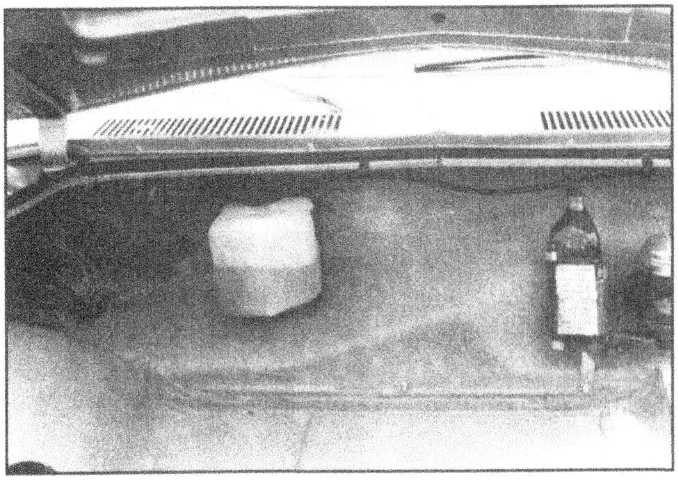

This 1965 luggage compartment shows the gray and white spatter paint pattern.

aqua and black spatter. The Willow Run plant changed from the white and gray to the aqua and black for the 1967 model year.

Mats for the bottom of the trunk were furnished for all models except the 500 series. Mats for the 500 models were available only from the dealer. The mats for the 1960 Monza and 700 models covered the floor of the trunk and extended part way up the side. They were made of rubber.

The mat produced in 1961 was also rubber. The bottom was black and the top had a black pattern on a gray background. It was much smaller than in 1960, covering only the floor of the luggage compartment.

Chevrolet changed to a cotton mat backed with foam rubber for the 1962 and 1963 models. The rubber mat with a black back and gray and black top reappeared in 1964. The shape of the trunk changed in 1965 necessitating a new mat, but the material and color combination remained the same. This mat was used in 1966.

In 1967 the color of the mat changed for the last time. The pattern and material remained the same. A checkered pattern in aqua over a black background complimented the aqua and black spatter paint on the sides of the compartment.

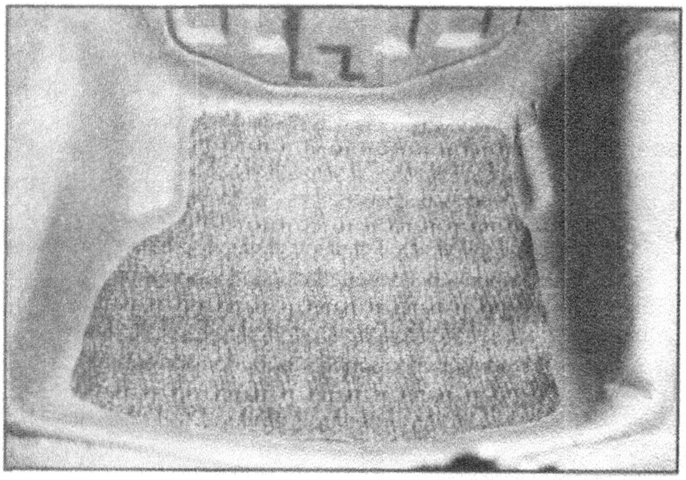

This is a replicated 1966 luggage compartment mat installed in a recent restoration.

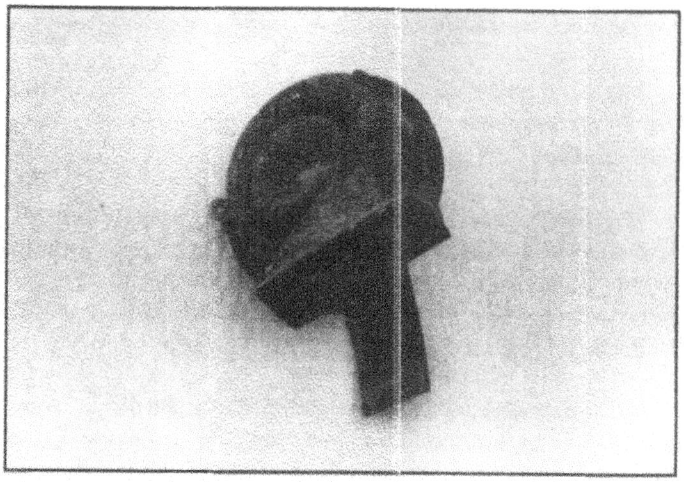

Delco Remy was the original equipment manufacturer of Corvair horns.

Horn

The 500 model had only one horn, while all other models had two. From 1960 through 1963 the horns were mounted behind the low beam (outside) headlights between the trunk liner and the fenders. The single horn in the 500 was mounted on the driver's side.

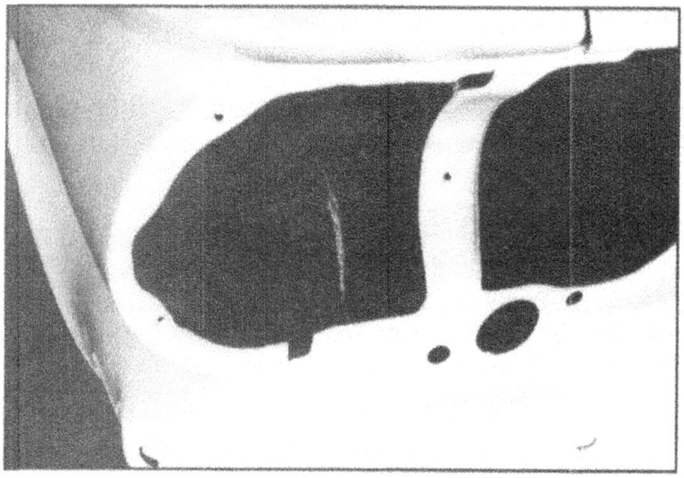

The horns were mounted behind the outside headlight. This photo shows the placement of the dual horn on the 700 and Monza models.

In 1964 the horn on the driver's side was moved forward of the steering box idler arm. All 1965 and later models had the horns located in the headlight assemblies. The horn in the 500 model was located in the driver's side light assembly. There were no external grille openings for the horns.

Tool Kit

The only tools supplied by Chevrolet were a scissors style jack and a foldable lug wrench. The lug wrench operated the jack and also was used to remove hubcaps and wheel covers.

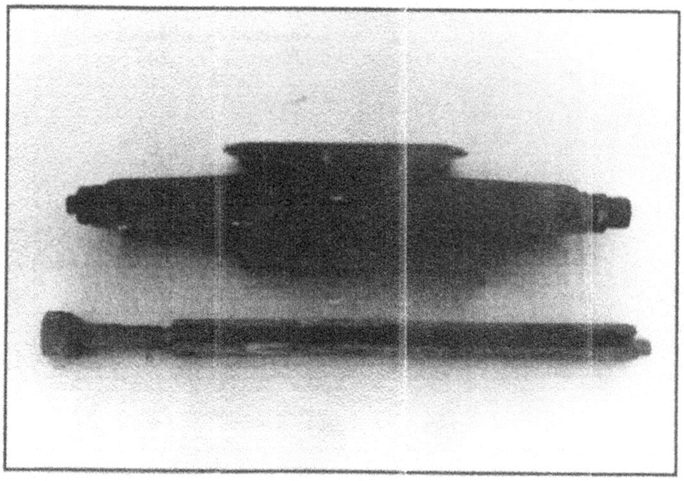

The standard equipment jack and lug wrench were stored in either the luggage compartment or engine compartment.

Jack support plates were located on the underside of the body just behind the front wheel and just ahead of the rear wheel. Bumper jacks were not recommended for use on the Corvair.

Chapter 3

Exterior Body Panels

Front Panel Assembly

In 1960 the front panel of the Corvair was concave.

The convex front panel was used on all models from 1961 through 1964.

Only three front panel assemblies were produced for all Corvair models. The first change came in the second year of production when the original concave shape was bulged out. The new shape added a little luggage room as well as a substantial styling change.

The radical styling change in 1965 prompted a major change in the front panel sheet metal after five years of Corvair production. The new style did away with the distinctive ridge running horizontal between the headlight trim.

No styling changes were made in the sheet metal front panel from 1965 through 1969.

Front Splash Panel

The sheet metal splash panel below the front bumper bar featured a series of vertical creases in the 1960 models. The same design was carried through 1964.

This 1962 Monza shows the early front splash panel design.

The major design change in 1965 smoothed out the splash panel. Another change was the placement of parking lights in the splash panel.

Note the smooth splash panel on this second generation Monza.

A spoiler was used on all models beginning in 1966.

Front Spoiler

In 1966, a black plastic valance panel was added to the bottom front sheet metal. It not only concealed the suspension but acted as a spoiler and helped stabilize the front end at highway speeds. The panel does fit the 1965 models and may have been added to some of these cars. Air dams retro-fitted to 1965 cars may be wobbly.

Front Fender

The front fender panels were identical for all models from 1960 through 1964. Emblems and bright metal decoration changed, but the basic fender design remained the same.

The 1960 Corvair 500 two door sedan reflects the early fender design.

In 1965, as part of the overall design change, the fender became sleeker with a less pronounced belt line. The bulge behind the headlight was removed.

This 1969 Corvair 500 two door sedan illustrates the sleek fender design that originated in 1965.

On the early models (1960-1964) the sheet metal covering the gas filler cap was located on the left front fender about 17 inches forward of the door. The 5.25 inch diameter lid was hinged to the front. A small indentation in the edge of the round lid allowed a finger grip for opening the gas cap covering.

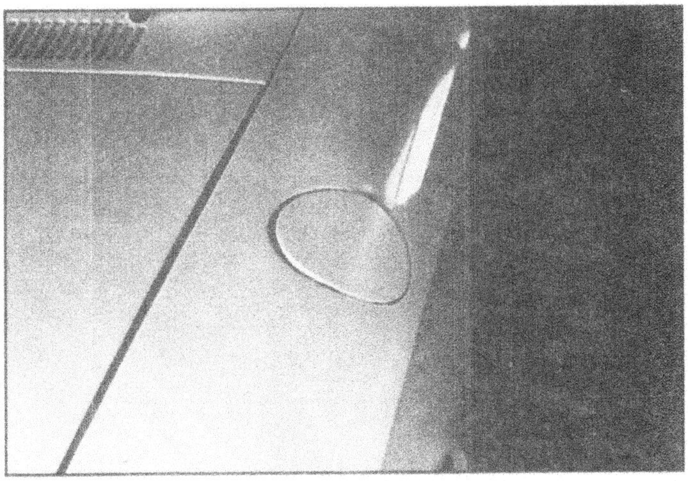

The round gas filler door marked the first generation Corvairs.

The gas filler door for the 1965 through 1969 models was also hinged to the front. It was rectangular and was relocated high on the front fender. The finger notch for easy opening remained.

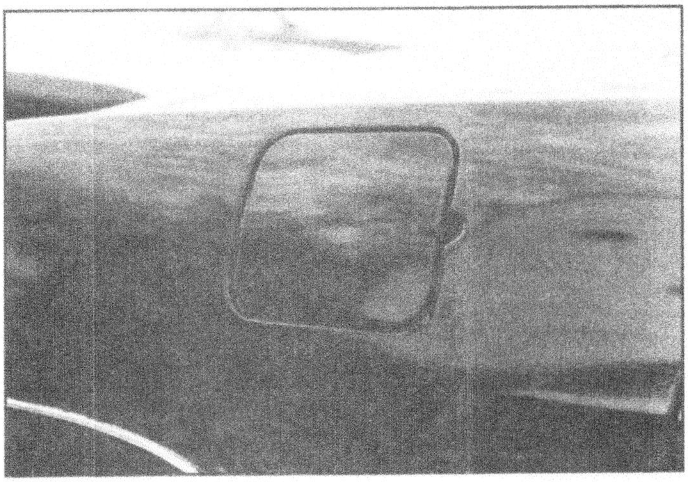

From 1965 through 1969 the gas filler door was rectangular in shape.

Deck Lid (Hood)

From 1960 to 1964 the front edge of the hood flared upwards at the headlights on each side. The lid was divided by a central ridge from the leading edge to the cowl.

The extensive restyling of the Corvair in 1965 resulted in a major change in the front hood or lid sheet metal. After 1965 the leading edge of the sheet metal was straight between the fenders. The hood had a more pronounced central ridge running full length from the leading edge to the cowl. The change in lid configuration made a remarkable change in the outward appearance of the cars. It added to the "cleaner" look found in the later models.

This 1961 700 model shows the pronounced flair of the deck lid above the headlights.

The crisp leading edge of the deck lid adds to the classic design of the Corsa.

Front Cowl

The front cowl had a grille stamped in it that was used to feed fresh air through the ventilation system. The design remained the same from 1960 through 1964.

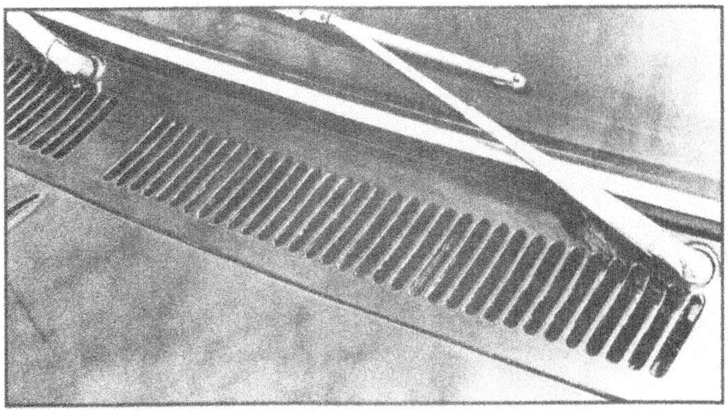

This first generation Monza front cowl shows the grille in detail.

The two grille openings, each 17.5 inches long and 2.75 inches wide, were centered in the cowl. When windshield washers were supplied, the nozzles protruded between the 16th and 17th bars of the grille, counting from the outboard side of either the left or right side grille. There were 31 bars in each grille.

A wider and longer cowl was one product of the 1965 design change. The cowl, measuring about 52 inches, was three inches wider than on the early models. Measuring eight inches at the widest point between hood and windshield, the cowl was about one inch wider than the earlier piece. A styling flair, a raised scoop between the grille and the windshield, was added. The actual grille was about one inch wider but three inches shorter than the early models. There were still 31 bars in each grille, and the washer nozzles (when supplied) were placed between the 13th and 14th bars on these models.

The raised scoop behind the front cowl grille is clearly visible on this 1965 Monza.

Roof Line

The roof (or scalp as it is called in the parts book) of the early two door model Corvair was clean and simple. The roof of the first generation four door model Corvairs had a distinctive overhang. This overhang was common on some General Motors cars of the period.

This 1960 500 model, with the price sticker intact, shows the roof line of the first generation Corvairs.

The stainless steel trim on the 700 and Monza series highlighted the overhang on the four door models.

The station wagons had a squared-off back. This gave the wagons a standard silhouette, although it was much shorter than other makes of wagons.

The luggage rack was a popular option on this 1961 700 station wagon.

While other manufacturers reserved the "hard tops" for the top of the line models, Corvair was the first to offer it for all models and all price ranges.

The post-1965 roof line was changed dramatically to give the car a more European flavor and a more streamlined silhouette.

The pillarless two and four door models offered an especially large expanse of glass area that gave the car a sophisticated look greatly appreciated by the public.

Convertible Tops

Convertibles were first offered in 1962. The standard top had to be folded manually.

The manual top mechanism on this 1964 convertible had "helper springs" for smooth operation.

An electrically driven folding top was a factory installed option. From 1962 until 1964 a hydraulic lift unit was employed to operate the convertible top. An electric motor and pump behind the rear seat provided the hydraulic pressure to operate the lift assembly.

In 1965 the hydraulic lift was replaced with a mechanical system. A small electric motor and reduction gears behind the rear seat turned flexible shafts. The flexible shafts supplied the power to drive gear assemblies on each corner of the convertible top. No changes were made in this unit for the remainder of production years.

Our information indicates the first tops came in black or white. They were made of a strong vinyl material. The dust cover, or boot, that protected the retracted top was color keyed to the interior of the car. It was also made of top grade vinyl material. The window was fitted with a zipper so that it could be safely stored when the top was retracted. Some information we received indicated that the original tops supplied by the factory for the early convertibles did not have zipper attached rear windows. The parts manuals we examined all showed windows equipped with zippers.

The second generation Corvairs were available as convertibles in the Monza series from 1965 through the end of production. The Corsa series had convertibles in 1965 and 1966.

The vinyl convertible tops were available in white, black or beige, while the boot continued to be color co-ordinated with the interior. It is interesting that any of the three colors could be ordered with any exterior body color. Chevrolet made no attempt to guide taste in color selection.

In 1968, white, black and blue tops were offered. The 1969 models came with only two color options, white and black, reverting to the colors offered in 1962. This was another indication of the production slow down.

Front Door Assembly

The first generation Corvairs had a distinctive ridge running the full length of the car. This belt line was easily identified on the door. The same basic sheet metal design was used on all front doors, although trim varied according to model and year. The front door of the two door models measured 47 3/4 inches wide at the belt line by 37 1/2 inches high. The front door of the four door models measured 38 3/4 inches wide at the belt line by 37 1/2 inches high.

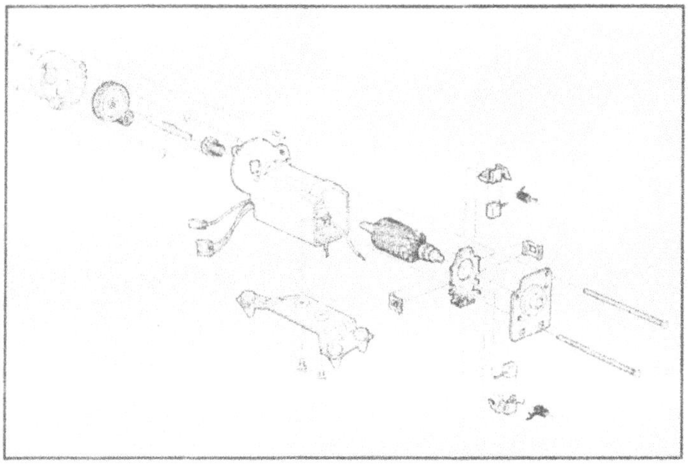

Page 14-1P of the 1976 Chassis and Body Parts Catalog details the late model convertible top motor.

The stainless steel strip accentuates the belt line on this 1960 700 two door sedan.

This close up view of a 1964 Monza shows the prominent belt line of the early body style.

The hinges used on the early models were the same design from 1960 through 1964. Of course upper and lower hinges have different part numbers as well as being designated as left and right hand.

The station wagon front door was the same size as the doors of other four door models, even though the roof was two inches higher. The hinges were identical to the ones used on all front doors.

The doors of cars produced from 1965 through 1969 reflected the complete design change. The distinctive belt line was subdued in these later models. The front door of two door models measured 51 1/2 inches wide at the belt line by 41 inches high. The front door of the four door models measured 401/2 inches wide by 41 inches high.

This photograph of a 1969 500 model illustrates the wider front doors used after 1964.

Rear Door Assembly

The standard 500 four door models were produced in 1960 and 1961. The deluxe 700 model was built from 1960 through 1964, and the Monza four door model was built from 1961 to 1964. The rear door of the early models measured 34 1/2 inches wide at the belt line by 37 1/2 inches high. The station wagons (1961 and 1962) were four door models. Once again, the station wagon rear doors were the same size as the rear door of all four door models.

Note the cut out on the rear door. Ignore all the non-stock components on this 1961 station wagon.

The lower rear corner of the rear door of both the station wagon and other four door models was cut out to follow the outline of the rear wheel well.

The 500 and Monza four door models were produced from 1965 until 1967. The cut out for the wheel well was not as pronounced in the post-1965 four door cars as it was in the early models. The rear door measured 34 3/4 inches by 41 inches high.

The rear doors of the late model Corvairs are visibly wider than those on the early body style.

This 1960 500 model shows the plain rocker panel as part of the unitized construction.

The two photographs of a 1964 Monza door and pillar show the early model door latch assembly. The latch was used on all two and four door models and the door was locked from the inside by pushing the door handle forward after closing.

Rocker Panel

Since the Corvair was Chevrolet's first effort at the unitized body, the rocker panel was part of the heavily reinforced body sill. It became part of the welded unit that included the front fender and the rear fender.

Unitized construction carried over into the new body configuration of 1965, and the front fender, rocker panel and rear fender were still one welded unit. These later models had galvanized steel rocker panels.

Lock Post & Latch

The original door latch assembly was used from 1960 through 1962. There was a minor change for the 1963 and 1964 model years. The latch was built into the front and rear door. The capture device was located on the center frame support on four door models. It was part of the quarter panel support on two door models. The capture device for the rear door was incorporated into the rear quarter panel support beam.

The second generation cars featured a forked capture mechanism. This new latch assembly conformed to the safety standards mandated for all cars of the period. The latch assembly and lock post location was the same as the early models.

Minor design changes were made each year, 1965 through 1969, and Chevrolet assigned different part numbers to the lock assembly each year. As with the door assemblies, there was a right hand and left hand designation.

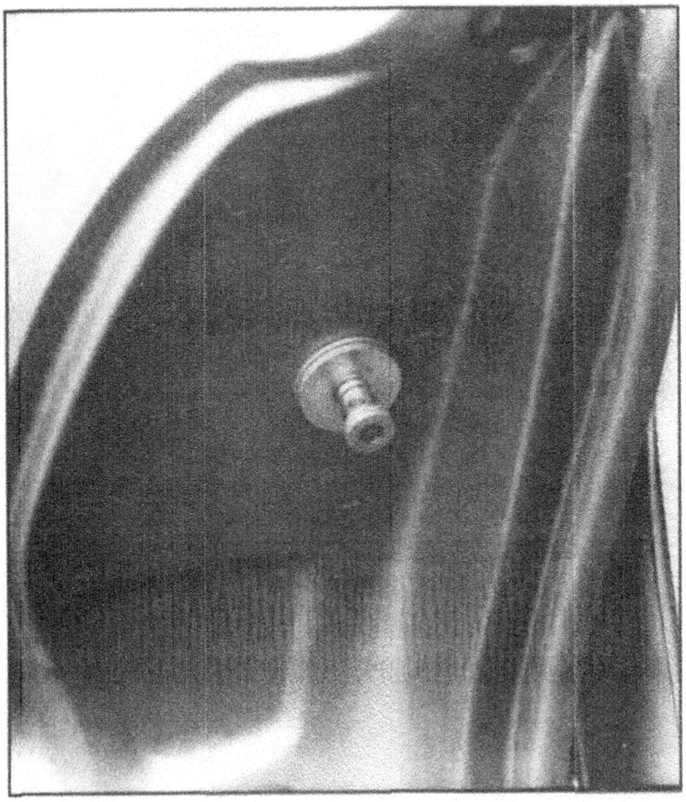

These two photographs of a 1965 Monza door and pillar show the second generation door latch assembly. This latch style was used on all two and four door models. The door was locked from the inside with a door lock button.

Rear Quarter Panel

As with most other sheet metal components, the design of the rear fender did not change from 1960 through 1964. In all of the early models the wrap-around appearance was very pronounced.

Straight from the production line, this 1960 Corvair 700 model clearly shows the wrap-around design of the rear fender.

The station wagon featured grilled engine air intakes between the belt line and the rear side windows. A series of five grilles were stamped in the sheet metal. Each grille contained seven vertical fins. The air intakes were on both sides of the car.

Engine compartment air was drawn through grilles in the rear quarter panels of all station wagons.

In 1965, the fender was given a square configuration that contributed to the entirely new appearance. The basic 1965 design was carried through the 1969 model year except that 1968 and 1969 fenders had holes in them for the marker lights.

The squared off rear quarter panel of the 1965-1969 Corvair gave the car a classic look.

In 1963 and 1964 the depressions for the dummy grilles were replaced by a flat panel.

Rear Cowl

In the 1960 through 1962 models the rear cowl between the deck lid and window was a single piece of sheet metal. Two indentations were centered on the cowl.

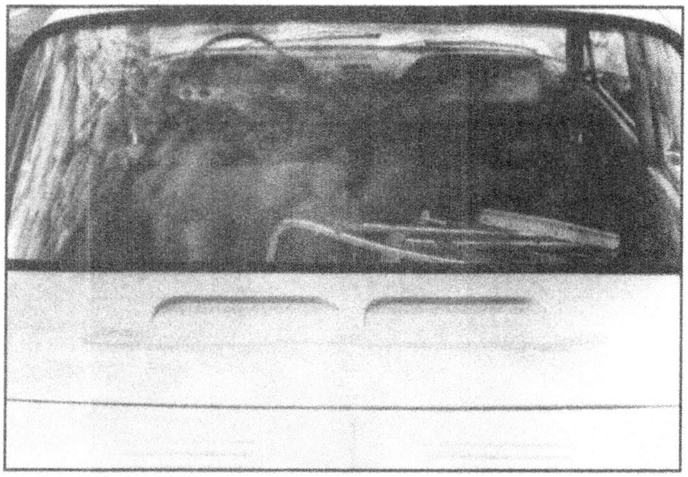

The rear cowl on the basic 1960 500 model had two sheet metal depressions.

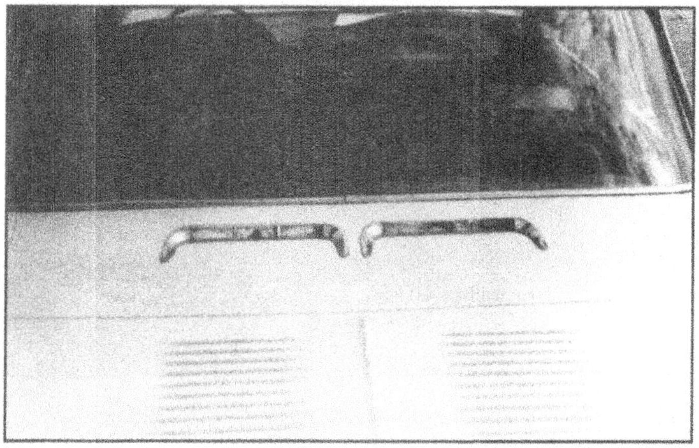

On the Monza series, the cowl depressions had bright metal trim.

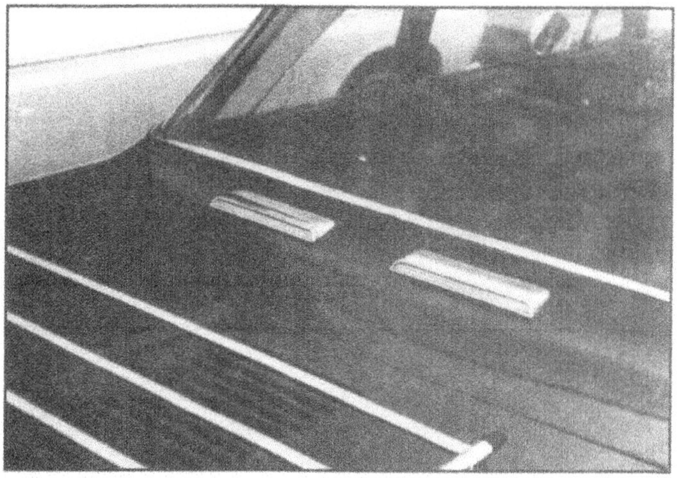

The decorative scoops were press fitted into the flat surface of the cowl.

After 1965 the cowl was changed to incorporate two grilles stamped in the sheet metal. These delivered air to the engine.

Rear Hood (Deck)

The long rear deck on the first generation Corvairs was the same for all models, except the station wagons. The rear deck had two rows of louvers stamped into the sheet metal. The louvers began just below the rear cowl and ended a few inches above the trailing edge of the deck. Each row contained 25 louver slots. The louvers added a distinctive styling touch to an already unique car and were functional as well.

The rear deck louvers delivered air to the engine compartment.

The designers attempt to put a new Corvair on the road in 1965 was evident in the new rear deck lid. The distinctive louvers cut into the top of the rear deck lid that marked the early models were removed. This lid design was used on all Corvairs built between 1965 and 1969.

Like the rest of the 1965 changes, the redesigned deck lid gave the car a lower and sleeker appearance.

The rear deck lid had double wall construction. A telescoping locking strut with a positive action lock was located on the driver's side of the engine compartment. It had a push button release mechanism.

The support strut on this 1961 700 model was typical of the lid supports on the first generation Corvairs.

The lid support for the 1965 through 1969 models was very similar to the one used in the early models. It had the same style positive locking device.

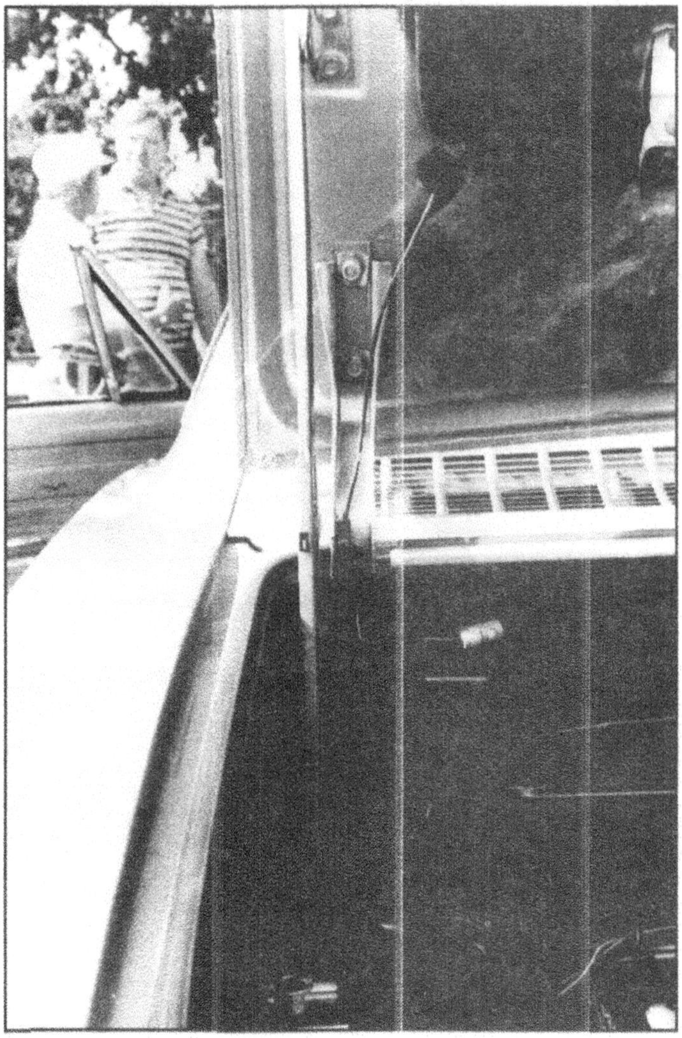

The lid support and thumb latch on this 1965 Monza was typical for all second generation Corvairs.

On the 1960 models, the liner of the engine compartment lid was one smooth piece of sheet metal. The spare tire was moved to the engine compartment in 1961.

From 1961 through 1964 the inner liner sheet metal had to be depressed to accommodate the spare tire. Also note the square lid lock catch.

Rear Deck Lid Latch

A spring assembly was used on the 1960 through 1964 models to put pressure on the latch. It kept the lid tight and eliminated annoying rattles.

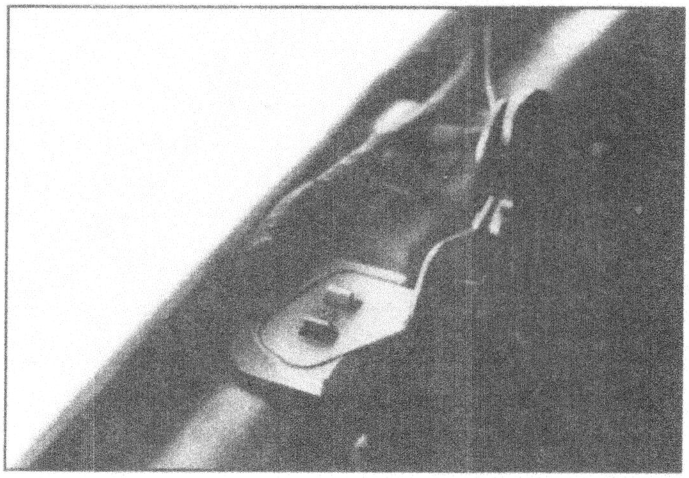

The 1960 through 1964 engine compartment lid locks were activated with a spring lever.

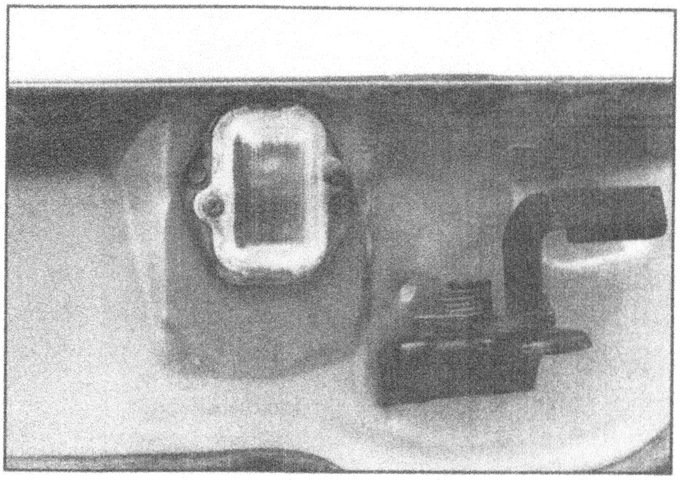

These two photographs show the engine compartment lid latches used on all Corvair models from 1965 through the end of production.

Rear Deck Lid Gaskets

A rubber gasket along the rear edge of the lid was used to help direct air into the fan and not let air escape between the deck lid and panel at high speeds.

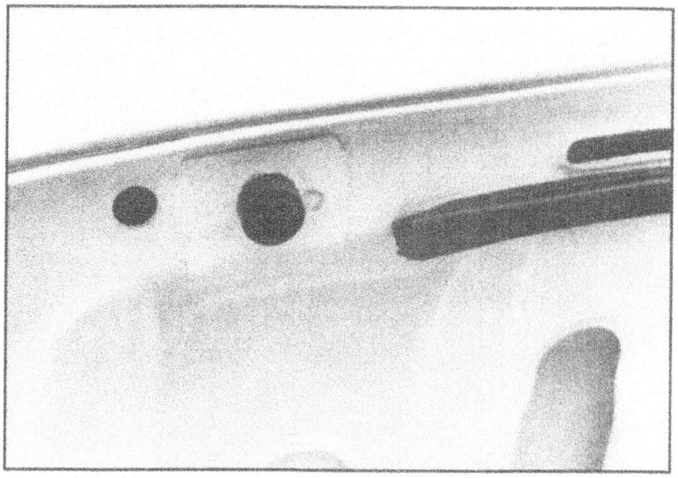

A short lid gasket was used on all models from 1960 through 1963. Note the lid bumper and drain hole.

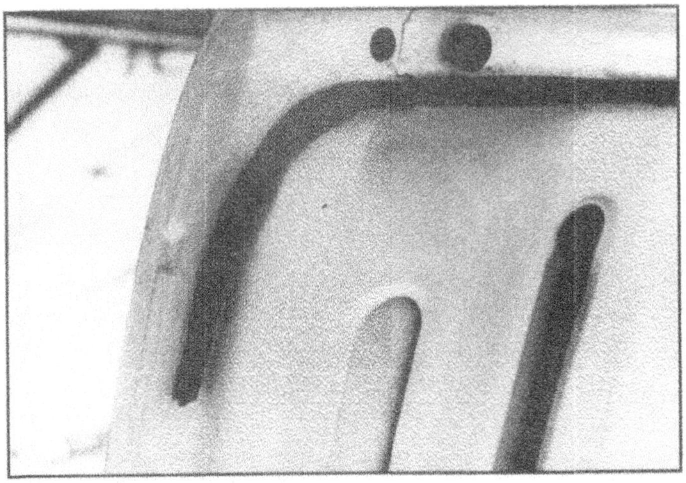

In 1964 the rear deck gasket was extended around the rear corners of the deck lid.

Turbulence prevented the exhaust air from being pulled out of the engine compartment. A gasket was installed in the body channel at the front of the lid from 1962 through 1964, to prevent air leakage and corresponding air turbulence.

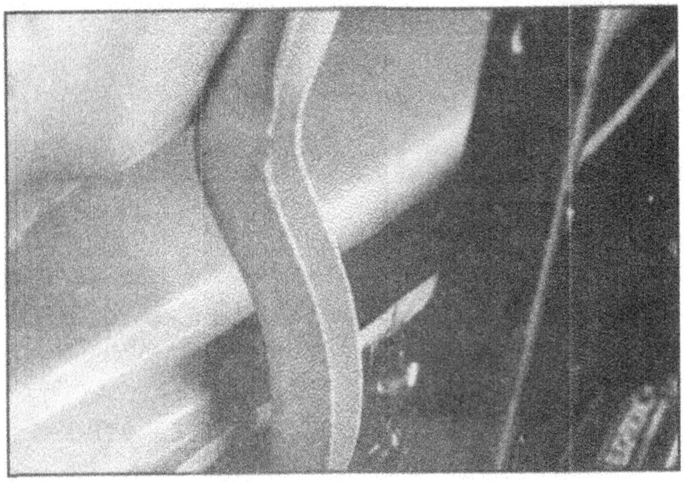

The rubber gasket can be seen behind the hinge.

The 1965 through 1969 Corvair used a gasket on the body opening that completely sealed the rear deck lid. The 500 models had no insulation pad on the rear deck lid.

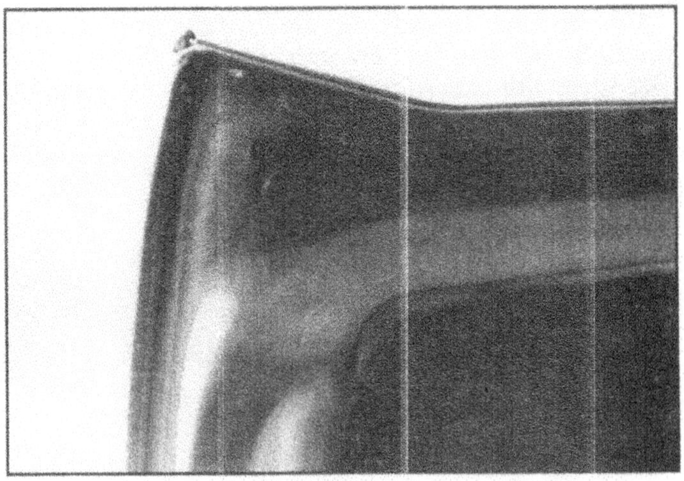

The rubber stop on the second generation Corvair doubled as a cover for the deck lid drain.

Rubber stops were used on both generations of Corvairs. They were mounted on the rear corners of the lid to protect from metal to metal contact and dampened noise. The second generation Corvairs had an insulation pad that covered the entire inner liner of the lid. It was fastened with clips that changed almost yearly. The 1965 clips were metal. Subsequent clips were plastic.

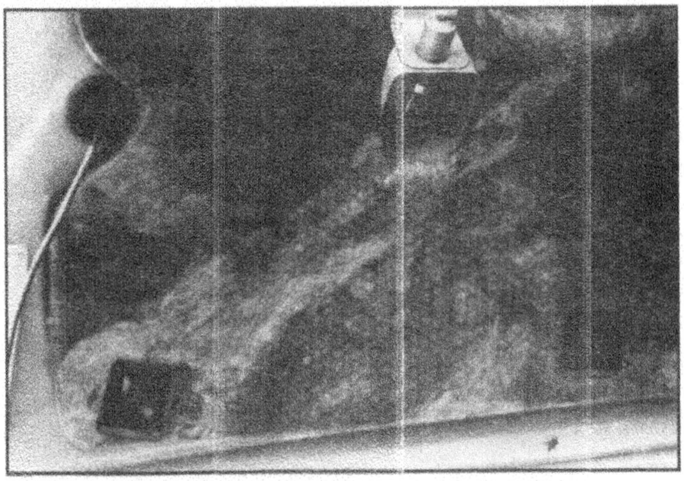

This 1965 Monza insulation pad (above) appears to be fastened with original clips. The 1966 Corsa (below) shows the clip design change.

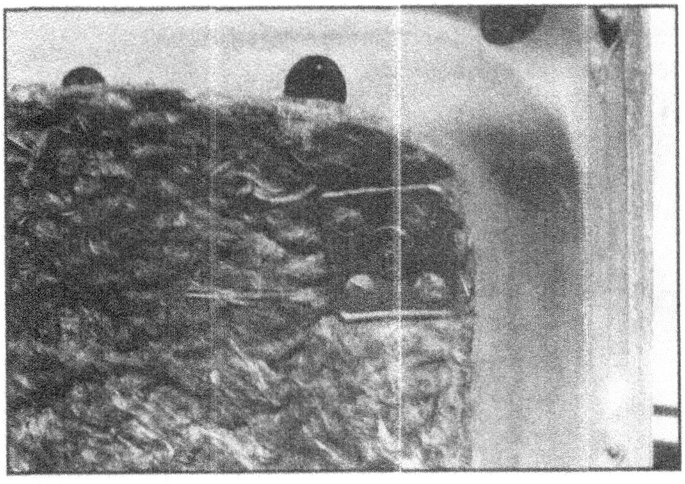

Rear Panel Assembly

The rear panel assembly, like the front panel, was a single piece of sheet metal that underwent one radical change in 1965. The 1960 through 1964 models had a wrap around appearance in the sheet metal between the deck molding and bumper. A recessed area housed the license plate.

This 1960 700 model shows the rear panel design that was used on all models through 1964.

In 1965 the rear panel was squared off. The indentation for the license plate was continued but was not as pronounced as on the first generation models.

The rear panel design, which began with this 1965 model, carried through the end of production in 1969.

Lower Rear Panel and Grille

The aluminum rear grilles on the early Corvairs were functional as well as stylish. The curved vertical bars were an exhaust vent for the engine compartment. They certainly caused stares by those unaccustomed to rear engine cars.

The tail pipe exited through a notch in the lower right rear corner of the air exchange grille on the 1960 models.

A small reinforcing strut fastened to the grille below the notch and strengthened this point. This design remained for the station wagons through 1962.

The 1962 station wagon (we found this one in Kansas City) still had the exhaust pipe exiting through a notch in the grille.

On all models except station wagons, the tail pipe was bent at a right angle in 1961. The notch in the grille was no longer needed, but some 1961 cars still had the notched grille. Apparently surplus grilles were used early in 1961 production.

The 90° tail pipe design, shown here on a 1963 Monza Spyder, continued through 1964. In 1962 and 1963, the bars in the air exchange grille were turned horizontally.

The 1962 Monza Spyder grille was identical in outward appearance to the other grilles, but used a reinforcing rod similar to the one used on all grilles in 1960. This reinforcing strut was also used on Spyders through 1964.

In 1964, the grille arrangement was changed again but continued to use the same opening size in the rear panel. The opening was divided into two equal sized sections each containing a mesh type grille. There were two sheet metal stone guards mounted behind the grille on the outboard sides. The stone guards were not interchangeable.

The grille design progressed from vertical bars in 1960, to horizontal bars in 1962, to the screen mesh shown above on this 1964 Monza.

The exhaust pipe on this 1964 Spyder was turned about 15° from the vertical axis of the car body.

When the 1965 models were introduced, it was apparent the air exhaust grille had undergone changes. The opening was still divided into two distinct sections but the total grille area was reduced in size.

The grille of the 1965 500 model was painted the body color. The Monza grille (not shown) was identical to the 500 grille but the screen was highlighted with silver paint.

The 1965 Corsa grille featured two anodized aluminum inserts. Note the sheet metal screws used to fasten one of the inserts.

The next year the design was changed slightly so that the grille was once again a single piece. The piece was stamped to give the appearance of twin grilles. The 500 grilles were again painted the body color, and the Monza was recognizable by the silver painted grille and trim. A one piece aluminum grille insert was used on the Corsa.

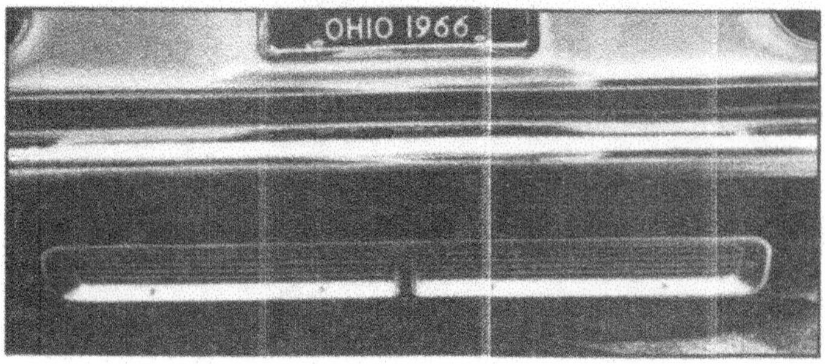

The grille design did not change in the remaining production years. The Corsa insert, shown above, was dropped with the demise of that model.

Chapter 4

Exterior Trim

Bumpers, Front and Rear

The front and rear bumpers on the model years from 1960 to 1964 were one piece assemblies with short wrap-arounds. All models used chrome plated steel bumpers. The front bumpers were interchangeable from one year to the next. The rear bumpers were also interchangeable from 1960 through 1964. The bumpers were not interchangeable front to back.

The front bumper and the rear bumper remained the same for all early model sedans and coupes.

The rear bumper on the wagon models was dished out below the license plate. The bumper depression allows the engine access hatch to open completely.

All of the bumpers were mounted with 3/8 inch chrome plated carriage bolts. On the wrap-around portion of the bumper the brackets fastened to a brace from the body rails. A bracket fastened to the chassis directly below the inside front headlights and a center bracket was used. The rear bumper was also supported at five points. The bracket assemblies were not interchangeable at any location. Bumper brackets were always painted black.

From 1960 through 1964 bumper guards were a factory option. The guards were distinguished by right and left hand models. The same guards were used in the front and rear. The bumpers and bumper guards were chrome plated steel pressings.

This 1964 Monza shows the early bumper guards front (above) and rear (below). They were interchangeable front to back but not left to right.

In 1965, when the Corvair line was redesigned, the front bumper changed in outward appearance. The wrap around was not nearly as pronounced and the support brackets were redesigned.

This 1965 Monza shows the newly designed front bumper.

The biggest change came in the rear bumper when each end of the bar was given a gull-winged look as it wrapped around the rear corners. As in earlier models, the bumper was attached by bracket assemblies at five points.

The gull-winged look on this 1969 Monza first appeared at the 1965 design change.

The second generation Corvairs could also be equipped with factory installed bumper guards. Different bumper guards were used for the front and rear.

The late model bumper guards, shown on this 1966 Corsa, were designed to fit either left or right side.

Turn Signals

The first generation Corvairs had the front turn signal/parking lights incorporated into the headlight unit directly below the twin headlights. The parking lights went off when the headlights were turned on.

The parking light lenses and bulbs were clear on the 1960 through 1962 cars. After 1962 the lenses were amber.

From 1965 through 1969 the front turn signal/parking lights were located in the front splash panel below the bumper. The lenses remained amber.

On the 1965, 1966, and 1967 models, the parking lights went out as the headlights came on. In 1968 and 1969 the parking lights stayed on when the headlights were turned on.

Headlight Assembly

From 1960 until 1964, the headlight assemblies had side by side 5 3/4 inch T-3 sealed beam lights with turn signal and parking lights immediately below the headlight unit. The headlight trim bezel for the 1960 model was interchangeable from the left and right side. This bezel was also interchangeable with the Forward Control trucks.

The polished aluminum bezel was a bright spot on this otherwise plain 1960 500 model.

After the front end was redesigned in 1961, the headlight bezel was changed. The left and right bezel were no longer interchangeable because they were flared on the inboard side.

This headlight bezel design was used in 1961 and 1962.

The 1963 bezel was the same shape as the previous year, but the area between the ribs was painted black. This painted version was carried over for 1964.

The only apparent change between the 1962 and 1963 headlight bezel is the black paint between the ribs.

Of course the headlight bezel design changed along with the rest of the car in 1965. The painted feature of the bezel was borrowed from the previous models. The flair design once again made for left and right pieces.

This headlight bezel design, shown on a 1965 Monza, was used on all Corvair models in that year.

The headlight bezel design was slightly changed in 1966. This change provided for better drainage, but is hard to detect on cursory inspection. A small trough was pressed into the bezel to channel away accumulated water. This design remained the same through the end of production.

Front Panel

There was no need for the front "grille" that is omnipresent in front engine water cooled vehicles. The Corvair had a relatively plain front panel. The designers at Chevrolet did not let that fact deter them from using the front of the car to signal yearly changes. The front panel exterior trim was changed almost annually. It is a key to identifying the various production years.

The 1960 model had a concave front panel that made it unique. The large Chevrolet red, white and blue wing emblem was centered on the panel under the teardrop lock.

In 1961, the front panel was redesigned in a convex shape that added room to the trunk. This basic shape remained through 1964. The emblem for 1961 was reduced to a small triangle attached to a slim horizontal trim piece that was mounted on the apex of the convex panel. The word "CORVAIR" was imprinted above the triangle. A red, white and blue Chevrolet bow tie made the emblem distinctive. The chrome plated teardrop shaped lock remained centered near the top of the panel.

The convex front panel first appeared in 1961.

For 1962, twin ornamental strips with black inserts replaced the single strip of 1961. These strips were separated by a small, elongated triangle just below the ever present teardrop lock.

The wide twin panel trim strips, separated by the large triangle, were unique to the 1962 Corvair.

Once again, in 1963, the front panel was redesigned. One single, long trim strip was installed on the apex of the front panel. This strip tapered to a point just short of the headlight bezel.

The 1963 front panel was highlighted with a new "Corvair" name plate and triangle in the upper left corner (driver's side).

A front panel molding similar to that used in 1963 connected the headlight bezels on the 1964 models. A white triangle enclosing a stylized Chevrolet bow tie was centered on the trim strip. The word "Corvair" in block letters was prominent on the front lid just above the lock.

On the 1964 front panel, the top half of the bow tie was blue and the bottom half was red.

Everything changed in 1965, even the lid lock!! A new one piece chrome strip was mounted at the top of the panel between the headlights. A triangle with the bow tie was centered on this trim strip. In 1965 the color of the triangle was red. The hood lock was hidden in this triangle. The word "Corvair" was written in script and mounted on the lower left corner of the hood lid.

Nowhere are the second generation changes more apparent than in the design of the front end.

In 1966 the last major changes were made in the front panel. The chrome strip between the lights was wider and flatter than the 1965 strip. The front lid lock was still hidden behind the triangle emblem, but the color of the emblem was blue. The triangle was compressed in 1966. The script name plate was moved from the front lid to the driver's side of the front panel. The emblem was flattened to fit flush on the panel.

1966 marked the end of the changes in the front panel. For spotting the difference between the 1967, 1968 and 1969 models, other features are needed.

Front Lid Lock

The front lid lock was centered directly below the leading edge of the front lid. The teardrop shaped lock assembly was mounted in raised sheet metal on the front panel. The location and design of the front lid lock stayed the same from 1960 through 1964.

The lid was operated by the key only and was spring loaded so that it "popped" open when the key was turned.

In 1965 the lock was hidden behind the hinged front emblem. Although the emblem changed in color, the lock design and location remained the same through 1969. The lid lock was once again spring mounted.

A small break in the Chevrolet bow tie logo was the only indication it hid the front deck lid lock. The photo shows a 1966 Corsa front panel.

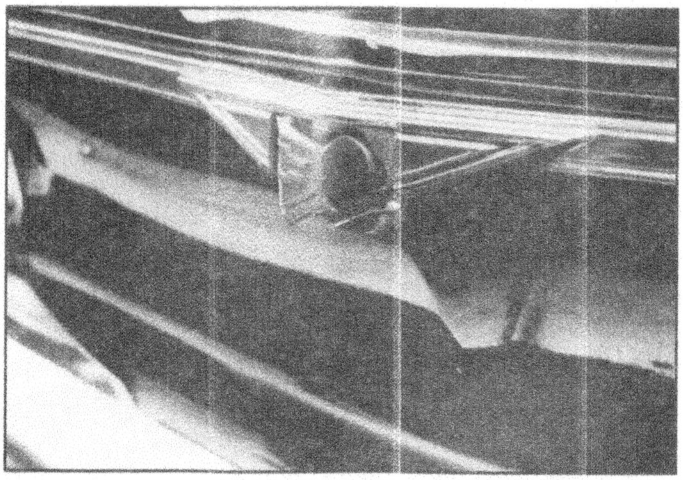

The lid was spring mounted and operated with the turn of the key. The same principle was used with the first generation Corvairs.

Cowl Area

No chrome or bright metal was used on the front cowl. The only ornamentation was the stamped fresh air intake grilles. Each grille contained 32 openings. The chrome plated wiper arms were fastened to a post extending through the sheet metal. On the drivers side, the wiper was located outboard from the grille and on the passenger side to the inboard. The 15 inch wiper blades operated with a parallel movement.

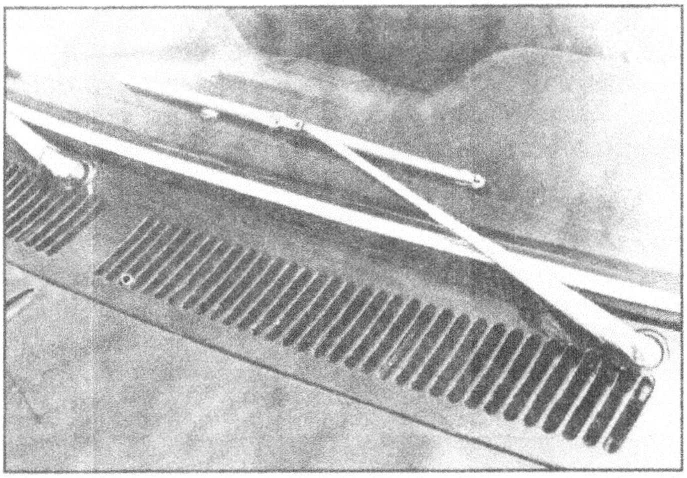

The front cowl grille was utilitarian. Fresh air entered the grille and was fed into the passenger compartment.

The 1965 cowl was noticeably longer. The stamped fresh air intake grille was incorporated in a depression in the sheet metal. Each grille still contained 32 openings. The windshield wiper post was located at the edge of the depression between the grille and the windshield. The wiper blades remained 15 inches in length and continued to operate parallel to each other.

The size of the cowl changed after 1965, but its function remained the same as with the early models.

Note the expanse of glass on this 1960 700 model.

Glass Area and Window Trim

The glass area was a basic design element and remained the same for all models for all years, 1960 through 1964. The windshield was of the wrap-around design which offered excellent side visibility to the driver

The most unique feature of the glass design was the wrap-around rear window of the four door models. This wrap-around allowed unprecedented rearward visibility and gave the entire car a wide open "greenhouse" appearance that attracted much favorable comment.

All of the first generation four door sedans had the roof overhang and wrap-around rear window.

The station wagons were different in design from the two door and four door models. The roof was two inches higher and the body longer. The interior was roomier and the silhouette entirely different from the other models. As evident in the photo, station wagon glass was altered to correspond to the body changes.

The glass area on station wagons mirrored their full sized cousins.

The second generation Corvair had a "wide open" appearance. This was accomplished by removing the side support pillars, curving the door glass, and significantly reducing the width of the stainless steel window frames on the side windows.

The removal of the side pillar gave the second generation Corvair a classic appearance still appreciated today.

Windshield

The trim on the windows corresponded to the model. The 1960 through 1964 500 series had no trim, while the 700 and Monza series had stainless steel trim.

In keeping with the economy design of the first 500 model, there was no bright windshield trim (above). The upscale 700 and Monza models carried the first hint of a sporty design with stainless steel windshield trim (below).

Tinted glass was first offered as an option in 1961, the same year air-conditioning was offered. If air-conditioning was ordered from the factory, tinted glass was also standard equipment. This combination of features remained through 1969.

In 1965 and for the remainder of production years, the windows continued to be trimmed in stainless steel on all models. This use of trim was in marked contrast to an overall corporate impression of understated elegance. Chevrolet was trying to move away from the gaudy chrome trim of their competitors.

Late model Corvair windshields were trimmed in stainless steel, even the basic models, such as this 1969 500.

Side Windows & Hardware

The Monza models produced from 1960 through 1964 featured stainless steel trim on all of the side window frames. This included a stainless steel molding for the center pillar and rear pillar.

This 1960 Monza 900 coupe was a hot seller in late 1960. One of several reasons was the sporty appearance enhanced by the stainless steel window trim.

The triangular front wing window (ventipane) was manually operated and rotated on a center pivot. This wing window was used on all models for all years.

The glass was held in a chrome finished metal frame. The outside latch plate on the early models was shaped to fit the latch. On the late models it was a smooth quarter circle.

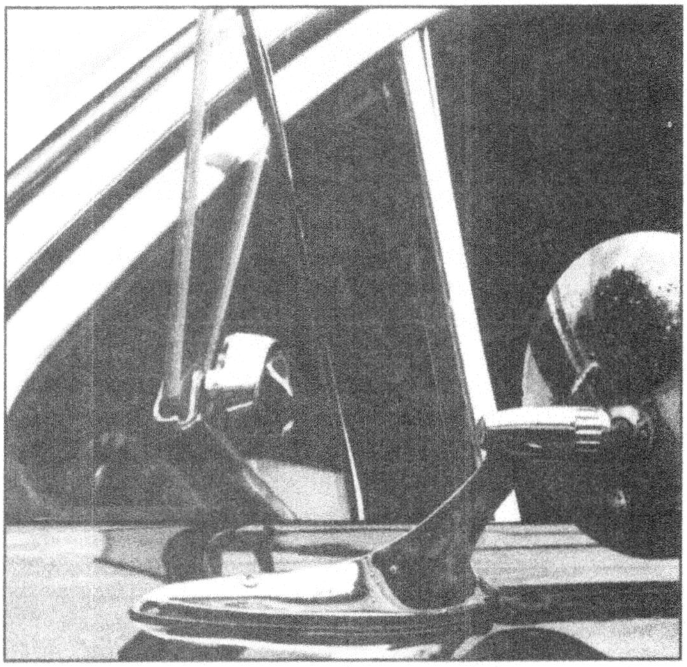

The chrome plated ventipane latch was hand operated.

All models of the second generation Corvairs continued with manually operated front wing windows. The friction latch on the 1969 models was considerably larger than previous years.

On all 1960 through 1964 Corvairs, including convertibles, the rear side windows were operated by a crank. The trim varied with the model designation. The 700 and Monza models had stainless steel trim while the 500 model had no trim.

After 1965, all side windows on two and four door models were operated by cranks, the same as early models. The size of trim on all windows was reduced. The rear side windows sported a narrow stainless steel band with attached rubber seal.

The hardtop design of all late model Corvairs is evident in this 1966 Corsa.

The curved, frameless front door glass rested against a rubber seal on the rear window, thus the hardtop look.

Rear Window

The rear window of the first generation 700 and Monza models was trimmed with a stainless steel molding. The 500 models used a plain black rubber gasket.

The rear window of the station wagon models could not be opened. This helped prevent the exhaust fumes from infiltrating the passenger compartment.

The rear windows of first generation Monza and 700 models were trimmed with a stainless steel molding.

All Corvairs built in 1965 and after, except the convertibles, had the rear window trimmed with stainless steel.

Side Emblems

Since the basic body style stayed the same from 1960 through 1964, and then from 1965 through 1969, one of the quickest ways to determine model and year of a Corvair is to look at the styles and locations of the name plates and emblems. To the best of our knowledge the exterior logos were chrome plated pot metal.

The 1960 models carried a connected block "C-O-R-V-A-I-R" on both front fenders ahead of the wheel well. The metal emblem was chrome plated.

The only distinctive logo in 1960 was on the Monza. It was placed low on each front fender, behind the wheel well. Belt line chrome trim readily distinguished the 700 from the 500 series and the designers apparently felt no emblem was needed on these models.

The Monza fender logo used in 1960 was distinctive for that year.

For 1961, the block letters "C-O-R-V-A-I-R" were removed from the front fender. The Monza once again had its own logo low on the front fender just behind the wheel well. The 500 and 700 series now had a nameplate on the front fender behind the wheel well just below the belt line.

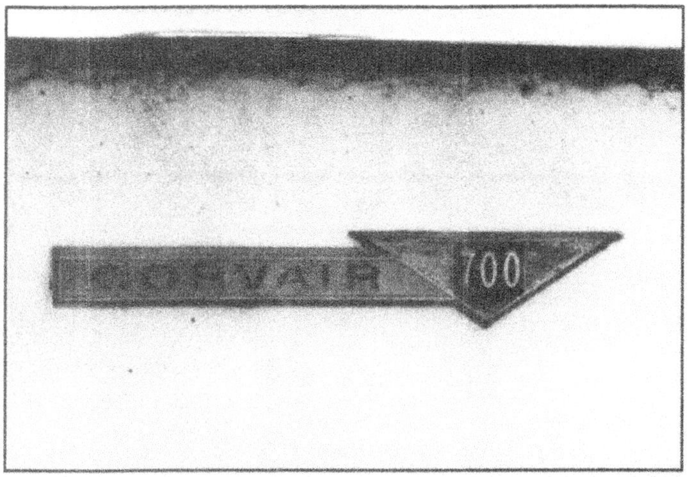

In 1961 the 700 series had its own fender logo for the first time.

The 1961 station wagon sported a script *Lakewood* designation on the rear quarter panel behind the engine air intake grille. On the 1962 station wagons this designation was eliminated.

This Lakewood script designation was used only on the 1961 station wagon.

The logo for the 700 series was moved forward of the front wheel well for 1962. It consisted of a block CORVAIR 700 between two trim bars.

The model logos were an inexpensive method of designating series and of differentiating between years.

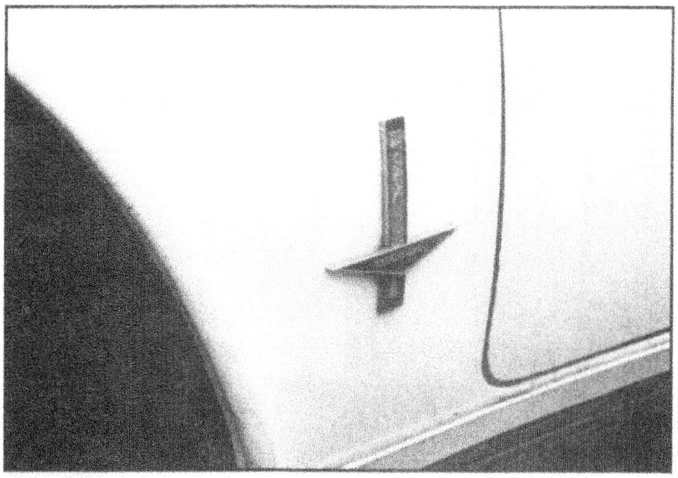

For 1962, the Monza logo was redesigned, but was still positioned low on the front fender behind the wheel well.

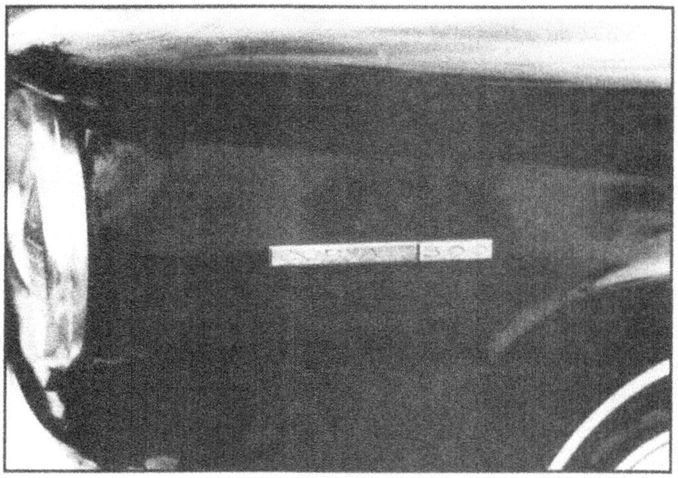

There were new name plates for both the 500 (above) and 700 series in 1963, and both were placed high on the front fender in front of the wheel wells.

The location and design of the 1963 Monza logo was carried over from 1962. The Spyder option was designated by the script "SPYDER" below the Monza emblem.

The shape of the 500 and 700 series emblems for 1964 was changed, but the location in front of the wheel well remained the same as it had in 1963.

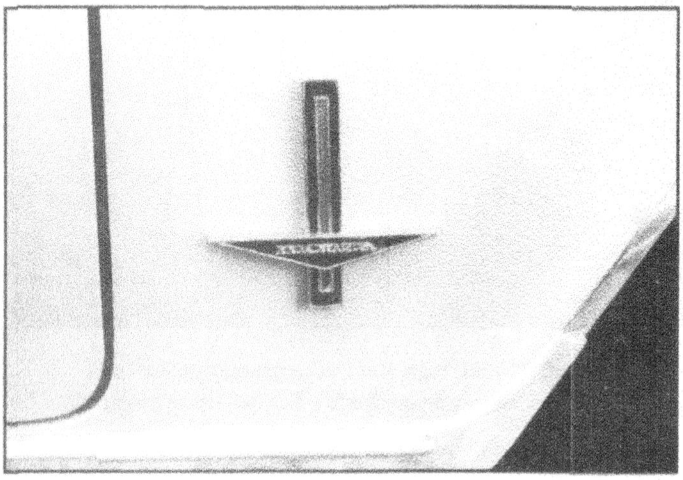

The Monza logo was changed again in 1964, however the location low on the front fender behind the wheel well stayed the same.

The round gas filler door opening was located on the driver's side fender. It could be fitted with a half moon chrome trim piece.

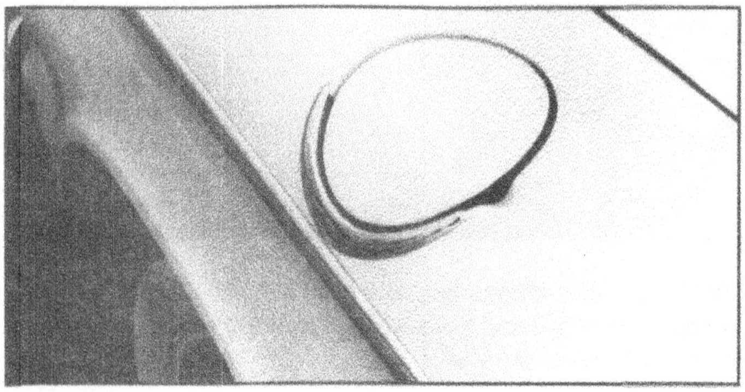

The gas door trim was available for early models. 1960-1964.

Not only did the silhouette of the Corvair change drastically in 1965; so did the trim decoration. The designers found a new cleaner look.

The gas filler door on second generation Corvairs was still located on the front fender of the driver's side, but was now rectangular. The chrome plated metal trim strip was retained as an optional feature for all models and years. It was mounted on the edge of the gas cap body opening. It was one piece that covered the bottom edge and extended up the rear vertical edge.

The 1965 Corsa model had a block name plate above and behind the front wheel well (above). Note the gas filler door trim.

The 1965 Corsa also had an emblem on the lower portion of the rear fender ahead of the wheel well (below).

The 1965 Corsa had pin striping the full length of the car. The single stripe was about 1/16 inch wide and was placed about 1/8 inch below the belt line. Pin striping was not offered in 1966. The location and style of the Corsa name and logo plates remained unchanged through the two production years.

The 1965 Monza side panel carried a single emblem low on the front fender. The emblem location stayed the same through the end of production, but the design changed.

The 1965 Monza emblem is easily identified by the split bar appearance.

The fender emblem on the 1969 Monza pictured above was identical to a 1966 Monza emblem.

In 1965 the 500 series had a model designation on the front fender above and behind the wheel well.

The model plate on the fender for the 500 series remained, but was changed in design in 1966. Instead of dark letters on a light background, designers put light letters on a dark field and eliminated the triangle.

From that point, the emblem remained the same through 1969 but the mounting system changed. From 1966 through 1968 the emblem was mounted with posts through the fender sheet metal. In 1969 the emblem had a self adhesive back.

There is no difference in the outward appearance of the 500 emblems produced from 1966 through 1969.

Radio Antenna

Radios were always an option for the Corvair. This may explain why a radio antenna was not often shown on the advertising photos of the car. The location of the standard antenna was on the right hand front fender, just outboard and ahead of the cowl. It was a manually adjustable, three section, telescopic antenna. It was supplied by the factory or dealer installed.

The location of this early antenna is correct. We could not verify that it was stock. Shown below is a 1966 Monza with a rare special ordered rear aerial.

Twin rear mounted manual antennas were first listed as a regular production option in 1964. The right side antenna was the live one, the left hand antenna for show only. The front mounted antenna continued to be available.

A new AM-FM radio was offered for the first time in 1965. This radio was only available with a fixed length antenna. Although this antenna was most often mounted on the passenger side front fender, it could be mounted on the rear fender as a factory special order. This same set of options were available through the end of production in 1969.

Wheel Well Molding

In 1964 anodized aluminium wheel well moldings were installed on the Monza and Spyder models. Wheel well moldings were unique to each fender. They were one piece and connected to the rocker panel molding. The wheel well molding was attached with chromed steel screws.

1964 marked the first year wheel well moldings were used to dress up the Corvair. They were featured on the Monza and Spyder models.

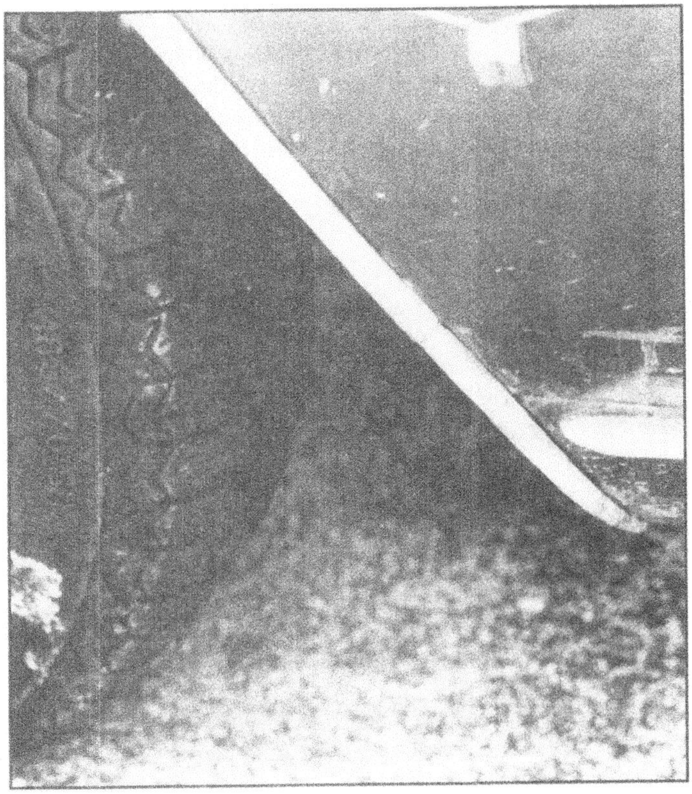

The 1965 wheel well molding unit (above) was ten separate pieces, four for each front well and six for each rear well. The units were not interchangeable between wheel wells. Well moldings were furnished on the Corsa and Monza models only.

The wheel well trim was narrower on 1966 models (below) than in the previous year. It was a one piece unit rather than several pieces. Wheel well molding did not change from 1966 through 1969.

Rocker Panels

The first two production years, 1960 and 1961, the rocker panels were devoid of chrome decoration on the 500 and 700 models. The Monza sported a rather narrow triangular piece of stainless steel that ran the full length of the rocker panel. The same trim piece was continued in 1961.

This 1960 Monza two door coupe was the only model with rocker panel trim.

In 1961, a rocker panel trim kit for the 500 and 700 series was offered by the dealers. The rocker panel decoration was not the same trim strip that was standard on the Monza. It is very rare to find a car equipped with this strip today.

In 1962, the dealer installed strip was still offered for the 500 model. The Monza and 700 series had a wide anodized aluminum strip covering the rocker panel.

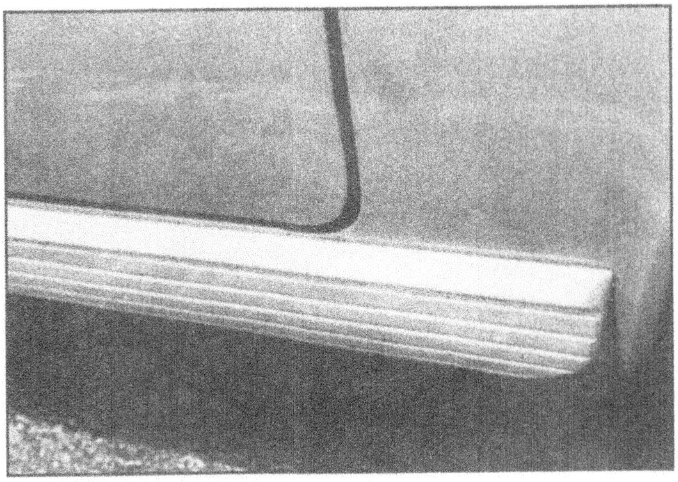

The 1962 rocker panel was the first of the wide design panels.

The major change in rocker panel decoration for 1963 was a matter of size. The rocker panel strip used on the 700 series was less than two inches wide. The Monza strip was the full width of the rocker panel. The design of both trim strips was similar, incorporating a series of wide bright ridges separated by narrow valleys painted black.

The black painted grooves were unique to the 1963 rocker panel trim.

In 1964, the rocker panel molding was once again redesigned for the Monza and Spyder. At each end a trim piece connected the rocker panel molding with the wheel well molding.

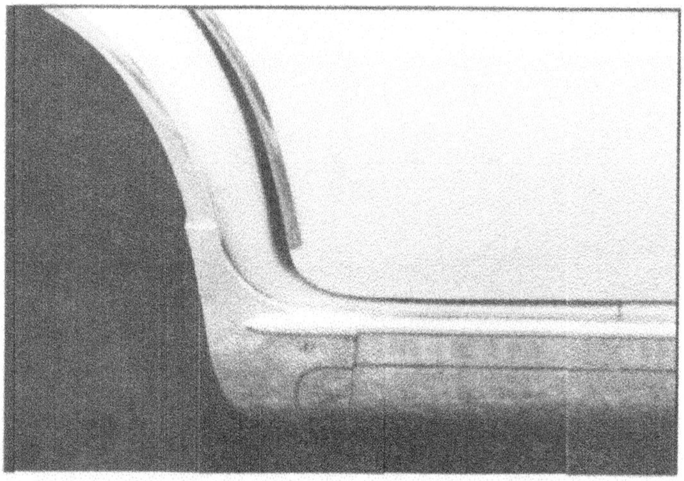

The new molding for the 1964 Monza and Spyder models presented a wide, flat smooth appearance.

The rocker panel trim on the 700 series in 1964 was the same width as that used on the 700 series in 1963. Designers removed the ridges and valleys and the piece was rounded.

The redesigned rocker panel in 1965 was graced with an aluminum strip that reached from the front to the rear wheel well. The trim was very narrow and looked much like the stainless steel strip used in 1960 and 1961.

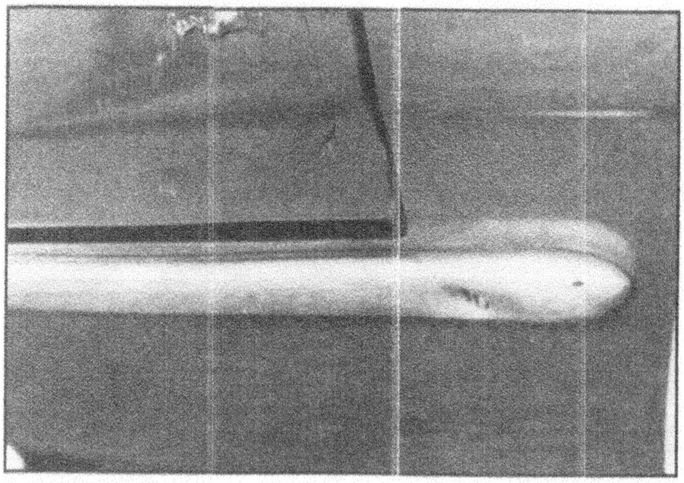

Rocker panel trim was offered only on the Monza and Corsa models after 1965. The mounting screw does not appear to be a stock item.

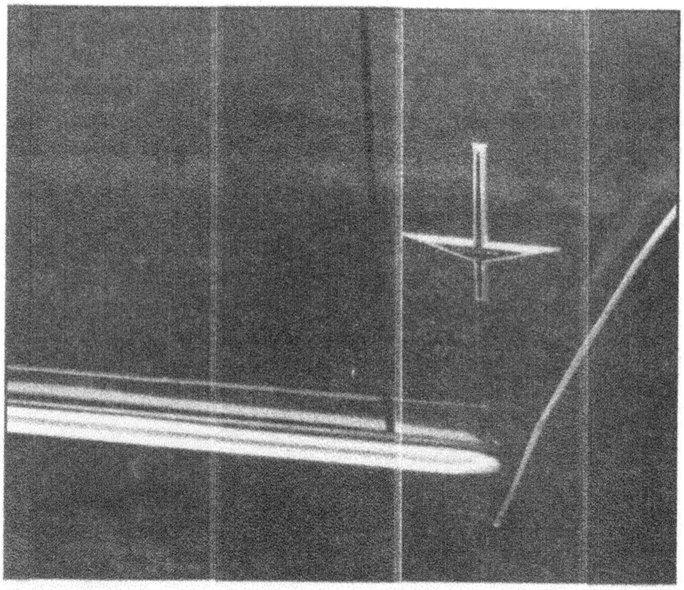

The rocker panel molding for the remaining production years (1966 through 1969) still had the narrow triangular shape. A flat ledge had been added to the top and to the bottom where the molding met the rocker panel.

Side Body Trim

The 1960 700 model had a stainless steel molding along the belt line. The belt line on the 500 and Monza models were free of bright work. The same trim scheme continued with the 1961 models.

This photograph of a 1960 700 model shows the belt line trim used in 1960 and 1961.

In 1962 the trim was modified so that the stainless steel strip extended only around the front deck lid, along the full length of the front fender, and terminated in the middle of the front door. The 500 was devoid of belt line bright work. The Monza shared stainless steel window trim with the 700 series, but once again lacked belt line molding.

The abrupt termination of the belt line molding half way across the front door was a feature of the 1962 and 1963 700 models only.

Although 1963 inspired no changes, 1964 saw major changes in the bright metal decorations on the car. The belt line molding was continued on the 700 series. It ran the full length of the car, as well as the rear, but did not wrap around the front as in earlier years.

Stainless steel door edge guards were offered as dealer options for all models for all years. On the 1960 through 1964 models the guards were installed below the belt line. On the post-1964 design they extended above the subdued belt line.

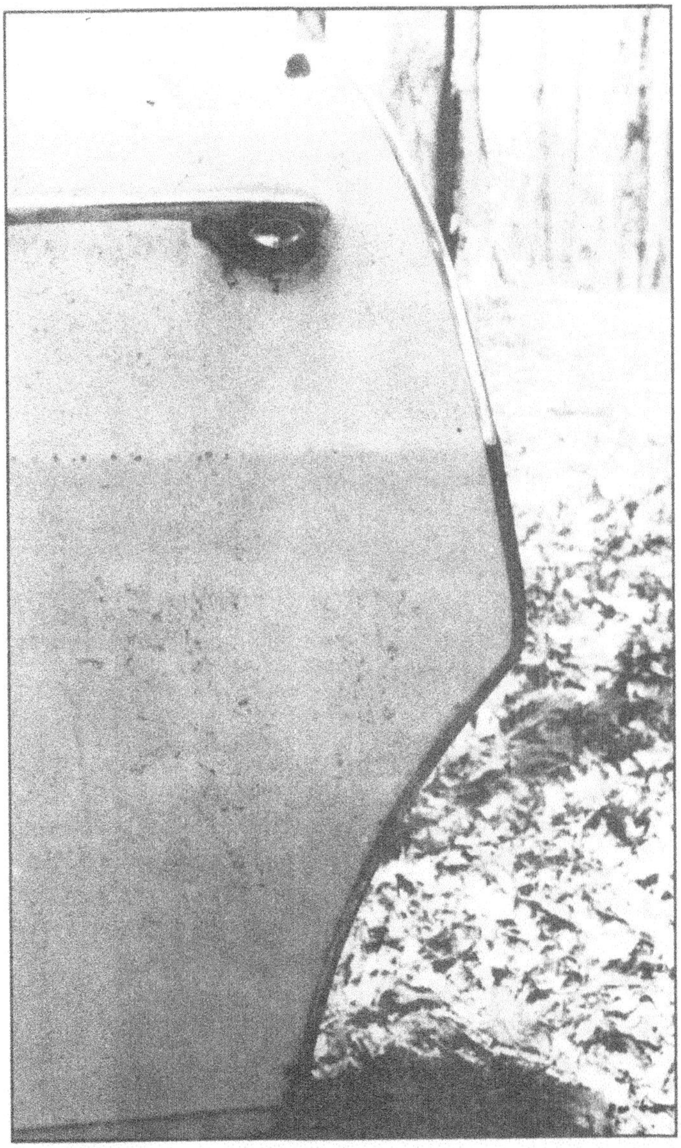

Door edge guards were a common add-on. To the best of our knowledge this picture shows a stock late model door edge guard.

The major design change in 1965 was reflected in the amount of bright trim used on the car. The belt line on the second generation cars was much more subtle and was not accentuated with bright trim. The body took on more of a "European" look. The only attempt at side trim for the second generation Corvair was the pin stripping on the 1965 Corsa. That idea was dropped after one year.

Rear View Mirror (Outside)

Until 1966 outside rear view mirrors were optional items. The 1960 mirror had a wide base and the stem or neck sloped toward the front of the car. It was anchored by one mounting screw toward the front of the base. A small bow tie logo was on the back of the mirror and the bow tie had a pebbled finish. The head rotated on a swivel on the top of the neck.

The 1960 rear view mirror had a round head and the mirror mount sloped toward the front of the car.

A re-designed mirror was used in 1961 and 1962. The entire mirror was more streamlined. The base was slimmer and pointed at each end. The stem was smaller and sloped toward the rear of the car. Again, a single screw toward the front of the base held the mirror. An elongated cylinder atop the stem held the round mirror head. The head itself was thinner, adding to the streamlined look.

In 1961 the bow tie design and glass size were the only rear view mirror features carried over from 1960.

Another design change for the mirror started in 1963 and would last through the 1965 model year. The base was made slimmer and took on the appearance of a two bladed knife. The attachment screw was moved toward the rear of the base. The neck still sloped to the rear. The cylinder atop the neck was shortened and sported a decorated ring where the mirror attached. The head was thinner than its predecessors and the bow tie on the back was enlarged as an outline with a smooth center.

This rear view mirror design, which began in 1963, was one of the few design elements that survived into the second generation.

In 1966 the outside rear view mirror became standard equipment on all models. The mirror head was the same as in 1965. The decorated ring was removed from the cylinder. The neck and base were squared off. The same mirror was used in 1967.

In 1968 the bow tie was removed from the back of the mirror head. Otherwise the mirror was similar to the 1967 version. This design was used until the end of production.

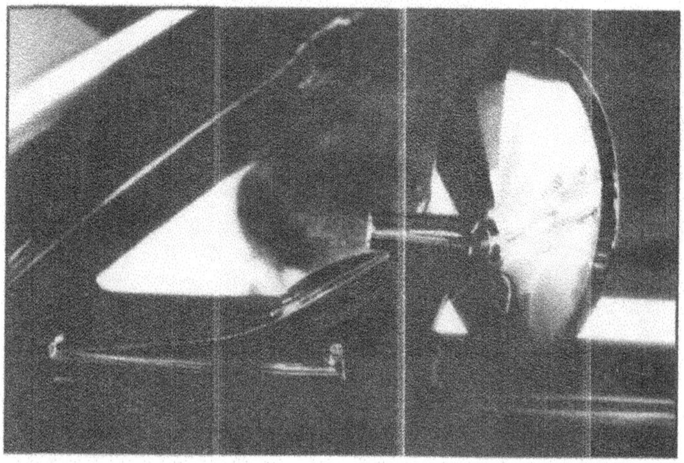

This mirror design has the least frills of any Corvair rear view mirror. Gone are the Chevrolet bow tie and the decorated cylinder.

A remote control mirror was first offered as optional equipment in 1964. The basic shape was the same as the standard mirror, but the base and neck was somewhat larger to accommodate the control cables. The interior control was mounted on the door frame and consisted of a simple black plastic knob mounted in a chrome finished plate.

The remote mirror offered in 1965 was the same as the 1964 model. The interior control knob was chrome plated to match the other instrument knobs. The plate holding the control mechanism to the door sported a raised bow tie. The installation was given a finished look by the addition of a chrome finished bezel that hid the mounting screws. This model remained until mid 1966.

Midway through the 1966 production year the remote mirror was completely redesigned. The head was now fixed, but the glass moved. The knife edge of the base and neck were blunted and squared off slightly. The cylinder that attached to the neck was made smaller and had no accent decorations. The neck still sloped toward the rear of the car and was held with a single screw toward the rear of the base. The bow tie was removed from the back of the mirror. The control knob bezel became a decorative screw-on nut. The designers were content to use the same mirror for the 1967 model year.

The remote mirror changed design again in 1968. The base was modified slightly so that it returned to the knife blade shape. The head was made rectangular. The glass still moved within the head and the bow tie was still missing. The single mounting screw was moved to the front of the mirror under the head. The interior control knob still matched the other dash knobs, but the decorative bezel was square to match the head.

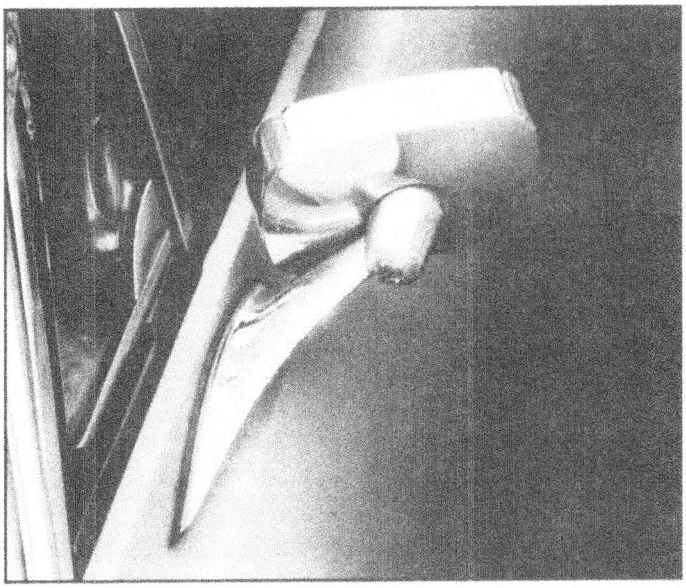

In 1968 the first square head remote mirror was used.

The only change in 1969 was to add a drain groove at the bottom of the head to correct a problem with water collecting in the head. Only the driver's side remote mirror was rectangular on the 1968 and 1969 models. If a customer wanted a passenger side rear view mirror and a remote mirror, the driver's side mirror was rectangular and the other was round. A rectangular passenger's side replacement mirror could be ordered from General Motors. These were the same mirrors used on the Nova, Chevelle and Camaro.

Front Marker Lights

In response to new safety regulations, rectangular marker lights were added to the front fenders for the 1968 model year. The marker lights came on any time the parking lights were turned on. In 1968 the lenses were clear with amber bulbs. In 1969 the lenses were amber and the bulbs clear. The lights were interchangable left to right.

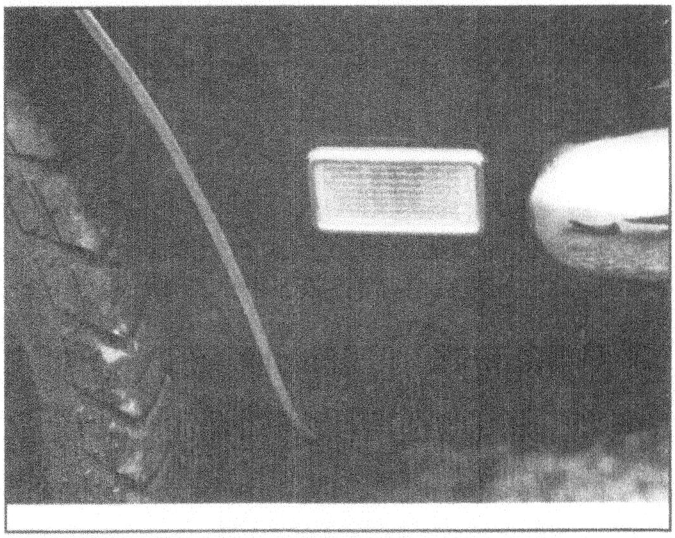

Marker lights on the 1968 models had clear lens and amber bulbs (above). The next year they used amber lens and clear bulbs (below).

Rear Marker Lights

Rectangular side marker lights were added to the rear fenders in 1968. This safety feature was continued in 1969. The rear marker lights operated off the parking light switch in the same manner as the front marker lights. These lights were also interchangable left to right.

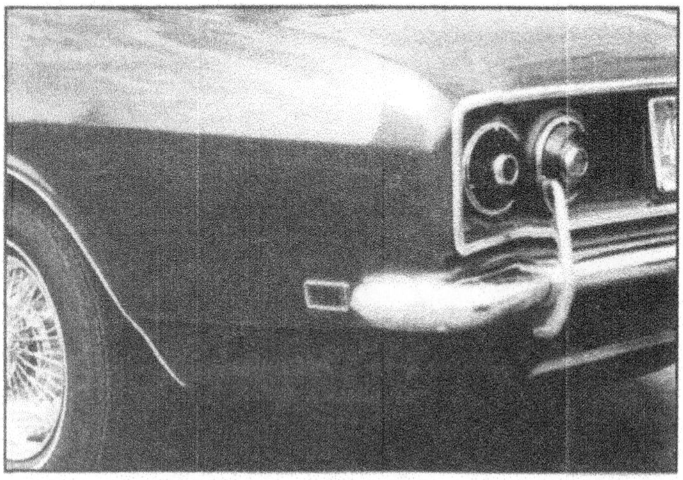

The rear marker light lenses were red for both 1968 and 1969.

Door Handles

The exterior door handles remained the same for all models 1960 through 1964. The latch button on the early models was round. The front and rear door handles were interchangeable. The 1965 through 1969 door handles had egg shaped latch buttons, but were also interchangeable front and rear.

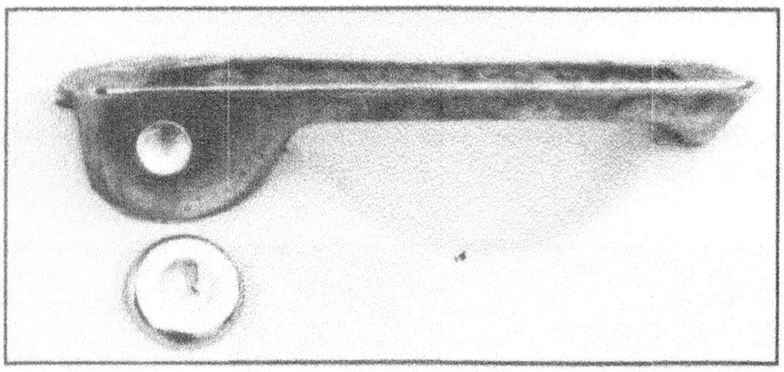

The early door handle is pictured above and the late design is shown below.

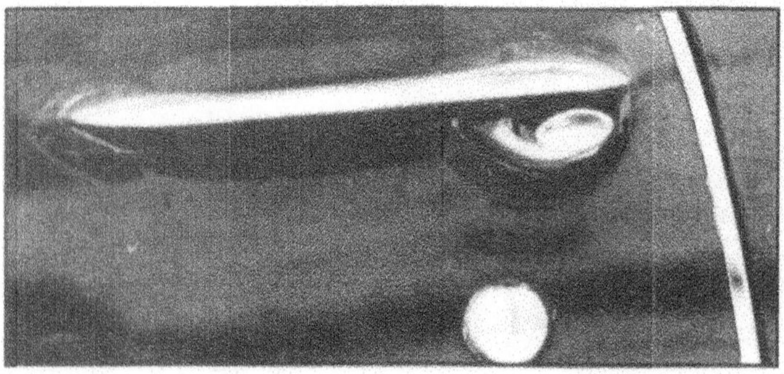

Rain Gutters

A rain gutter was furnished on all models except the convertibles. The gutter was painted metal on the 500 series. It was trimmed in stainless steel on all other models from 1960 through 1969.

A stainless steel rain gutter was used on the more expensive solid top models.

Rear Lid

The markings on the rear lid are a key to identifying several different years. The 1960 models carried connected block "CHEVROLET" letters on the rear lid.

The deck lid on the 1960 models carried simple chrome plated block letters.

In 1961, the "CHEVROLET" letters were gone from the rear deck. Instead, the rear deck carried a small Corvair triangle.

An emblem featuring block "CORVAIR" letters, connected by a single bar, was placed on the rear deck of all Corvairs for 1962. The engine size was designated on the rear lid of the Corvair.

If the high performance 102 H.P. engine was ordered, a special emblem was added to the rear deck nameplate.

The same "CORVAIR" name plate was used in 1963. If the new 150 turbocharged engine or 102 high performance was installed, a special logo was placed under the name. The same turbocharged logo was used in 1963 and 1964.

This unique turbocharged emblem was used on Spyders in 1963 and 1964.

The lettering on the rear deck of the 1964 Corvair was changed to look very much like the lettering on the front lid. Engine designation were centered below the lettering.

The unconnected block letters on the rear deck of the 1964 models were clean and simple.

The rear deck lid of the 1965 model carried a script "*Corvair* " in the lower right corner. The engine designation was located at the lower center of the lid.

This script nameplate was used on all models from 1965 through 1969.

These engine designation plates were used in 1965.
Top: 110 H.P.
Middle: 140 H.P.
Bottom: Turbocharged 180 H.P.

The script name remained in 1966, but the horse-power logos were changed slightly. The 140 and 180 H.P. engines were not produced after 1966.

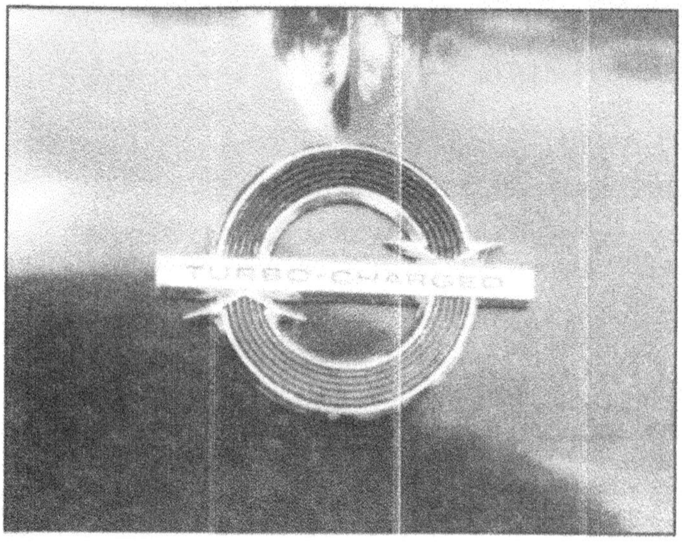

The engine plates shown above were used in 1966.
Top: 110 H.P. (1966-1969)
Middle: 140 H.P.
Bottom: 180 H.P.

Rear Panel

In 1963 a chrome plated bezel was added to the license plate recess on the 700 and Monza series. This bezel was offered on the 1963 and 1964 models, but was not incorporated in the 1965 styling change.

The chrome plated bezel for the license plate niche was offered only on the 1963 and 1964, 700 and Monza series.

The bright metal trim was noticeably absent from the rear panel on the early Corvair models. It wasn't until the second generation that the designers put the finishing touch to the top of the line models. The rear panel of the 500 series had no trim but the Monza and Corsa had a trim border to set off the new squared panel.

The rear panel of this 1965 Monza was set off with a bright trim border. This trim carried through 1969.

The Corsa was even more distinctive with a silver painted rear panel in addition to the bright trim.

Rear Light Group

Simple combination stop/tail lights were offered on the first model Corvairs. The center of the plastic lens was slightly raised with a thin bright metal rim for accent. The model year is molded into all rear light lenses 1960 through 1969.

Provision was made for back up lights that were optional on the 500 and 700 models. When they were not installed, the holes in the sheet metal were covered with aluminum inserts shaped like the missing lenses.

The photograph above shows the 1960 backup light covers.

The upscale 1960 Monza model had a slightly fancier tail light and it came with backup lights as standard equipment.

The same tail light appearance carried over to the 1961 models, but the light socket was redesigned. The bulb was positioned vertically instead of horizontally. This did away with the large hole in the body needed to change the bulbs of the 1960 models.

This 1961 700 model was equipped with the optional back up lights.

The method of supplying electric current to the lights in the rear hatch was an interesting feature of the station wagons. Two bare metal strips, one in the frame of the hatch and one on the side of the hatch, made contact when the hatch was closed.

Close inspection will reveal the electrical contact strip on the hatch of this 1962 station wagon.

In 1962, the design of the rear lights was changed. The plastic lenses were enlarged and flattened. A double trim ring was added to both the backup light and the tail light. The clear center of the backup lens was surrounded by a red outer ring. The stop/tail light lens was solid red.

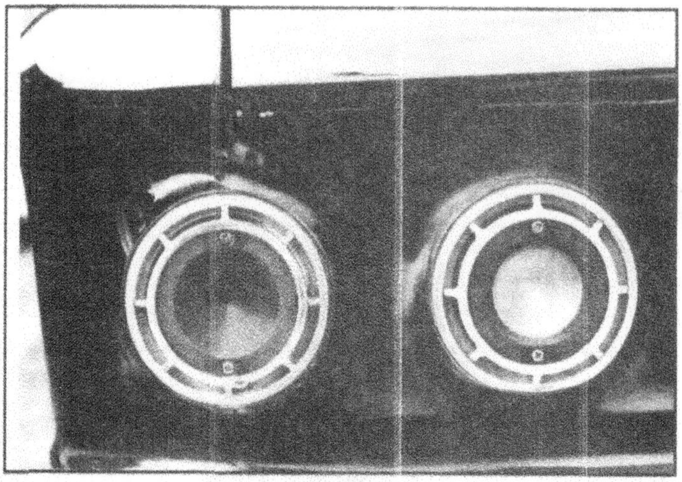

The large, connected double rings of the 1962 tail light lens added a splash of trim to the rear panel.

In 1963 both the back up and tail lights were split by a vertical aluminum "fin" which attached to an inner and outer trim ring.

The rear lights changed slightly in 1964. The vertical bar was eliminated but a small horizontal bar connected the inner and outer trim ring. The backup lens continued the now familiar clear center and red outer ring.

One of the trim changes made in 1964 was the restyling of the rear light group.

With all of the major changes evident in 1965, the rear lights had to be completely redesigned. The lights were more streamlined. Housings were one piece stampings and the lens fitted into a raised lip in the rear panel. A single trim ring decorated both lenses. The lens featured an elongated center encased in a trim ring. Throughout the 1965 production year a large diameter trim ring was used.

Back-up lights were still optional equipment on the 500 model in 1965.

Back-up lights became standard equipment on all models in 1966 when they were mandated by the Department of Transportation. The 1966 tail lights were distinguished by a thin aluminum trim ring, much smaller in diameter than the previous year. The center and the outside ring of the backup lenses were red, leaving just a small interior clear ring.

The early 1966 tail lights had the narrow band shown here. A change in mid-year resulted in some 1966 cars being fitted with the wide band lights shown below.

The 1967 rear light group, installed as a running change in 1966, is identified by the wide band of bright metal on the interior ring. This is sometimes refered to as the "wedding ring".

The change made in mid-1966 to the rear light lens was the last one. This lens was used until the end of production.

License Plate Lights

The license plate light was located in the overhang area above the license plate recess in the early Corvairs. In 1960 the light lens was made of glass. In 1961 the lens was removed completely. The connections were protected from moisture by a rubber jacket protecting all exposed parts.

Station wagons used a two bulb arrangement. The twin housings were painted the body color and were mounted on either side of the license plate. The same arrangement continued for the 1962 wagons.

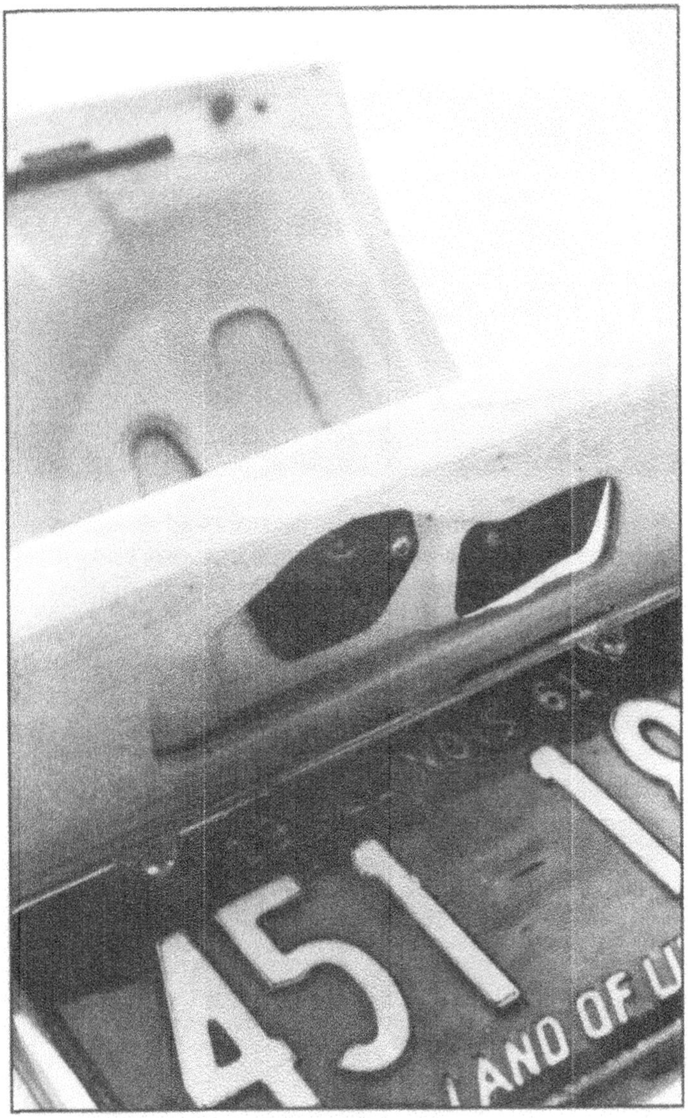

Unlike 1960, when a lens protected the license plate light, there was no lens in 1961. The electric socket was encased in rubber to keep out moisture.

Protruding horns enclosed the license plate lights on the station wagons. They were easily damaged when the engine access door was opened.

In 1963, a clear plastic lens and gasket was added to the license plate light. The light unit did not change again until 1965.

In 1965 the surface of the lens was changed twice in an effort to get better light diffusion. The first lens produced had vertical lines in the clear plastic. A mid- year change resulted in a lens with horizontal lines. No further changes in the license plate light were made through the end of production.

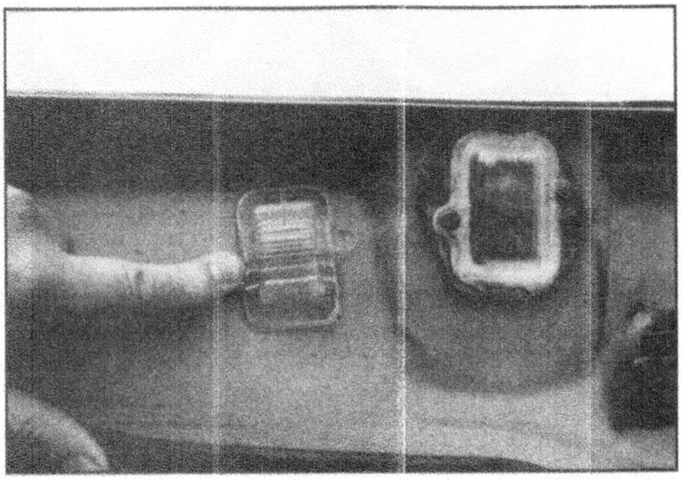

The original 1965 lens is on the car. The mid-year change is to the left. Note the spacing of the diffusion lines.

Hubcaps and Wheel Covers

We viewed several hundred cars, and the item most often incorrect were the wheel covers. We have included the chart from the Chevrolet Parts book to help clear up the confusion, but admit we still may have made some misidentifications based on information supplied to us.

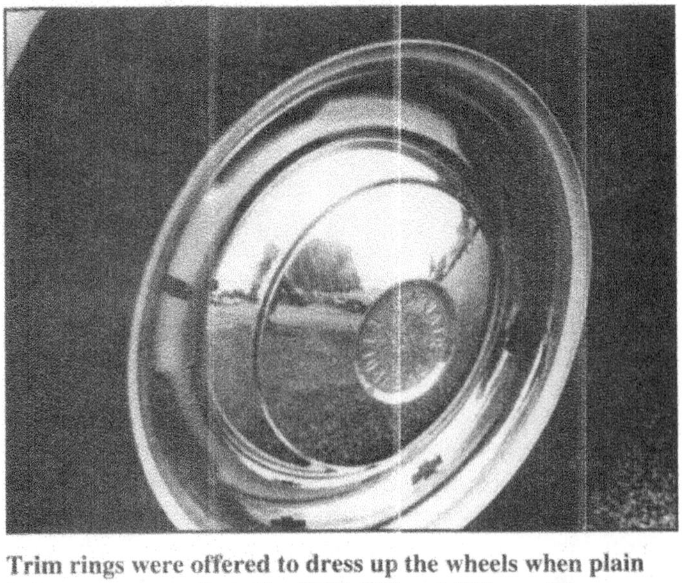

Trim rings were offered to dress up the wheels when plain hubcaps were used on the 1960, 500 and 700. models.

In 1960, the basic 500 series and the more luxurious 700 models came with the standard hubcaps. The hubcaps were very plain and distinctly convex. Chrome trim rings were offered to dress up the wheels.

Sometime during 1960 the convex shape of the standard hubcap was flattened. The convex shape made the hubcap subject to damage when the car was parked too close to a high curb.

The late arriving 1960 Monza came equipped with full wheel covers as standard equipment. The covers sported a cone shaped center.

The late 1960 model hubcap and trim ring was offered as standard equipment for the 1961 500 and 700 series.

Newly styled full wheel covers, still standard on the Monza, were offered as options on the other models in 1961.

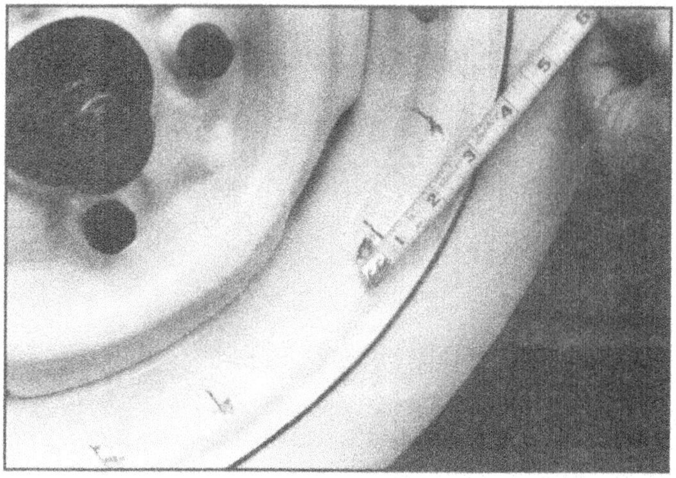

1961 was the only year that small protrusions anchored the wheel covers.

A newly designed 1962 wheel cover was once again a standard offering on the Monza, and an option on the lesser models.

The 500 and 700 models were offered with a redesigned hubcap for 1962. The trim rings were not offered. Many owners ordered the optional wheel covers to dress up the 500 and 700 models.

The design of these wheel covers was innovative because the center consisted of a plastic insert that could be changed. This allowed the same basic wheel cover to be used on any car with only the insert changed to denote the various models.

Wire wheel covers with two spinner bars were offered as an option to dress up all 1962 models.

Real wire wheels became available as an option for all models in 1962. The center had the familiar bow tie and the word "Chevrolet" showed on the hub ring. Selling for $269.00, they were manufactured by Kelsey-Hayes. Mounting adapters, knock off spinners, and a lead hammer were included.

The only wheel cover change in 1963 was to add a black accent color. This old hucap shows considerale fading.

In 1964 the wheel covers were extensively restyled. Since the entire car was redesigned in 1965, the 1964 versions became unique. The 500 and 700 models still came with a hubcap as standard equipment.

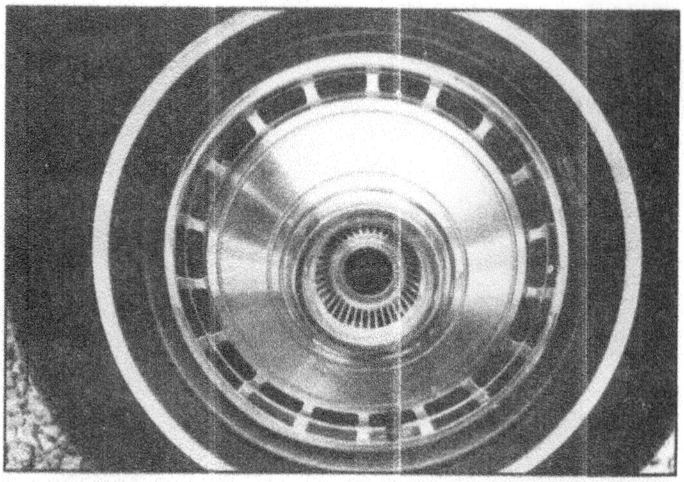

The optional wheel covers still used the interchangeable inserts with the Monza insert carrying the word "MONZA" and the 500 and 700 models having a bow tie in a triangle.

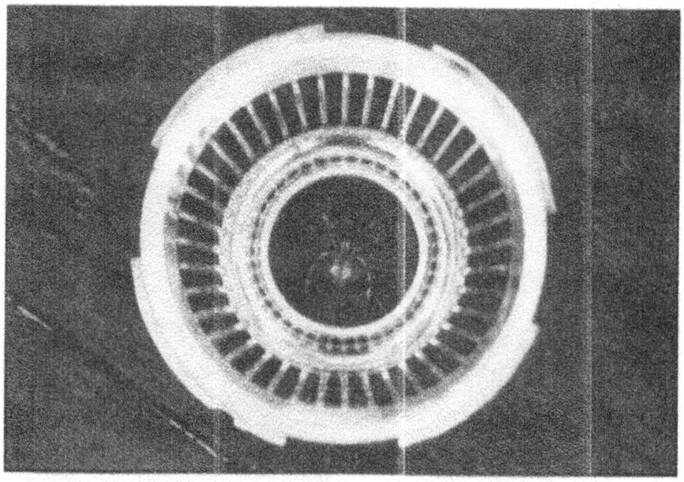

The wheel cover inserts for the 1964 Spyder were special. They displayed a large gold spider on a black background.

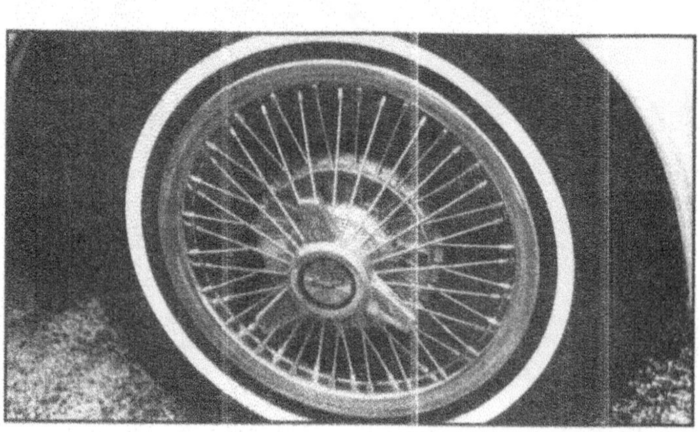

Simulated wire wheels with a three bar spinner were optional equipment in 1964.

Kelsey Haynes real wire wheels continued as an option in 1964. They were shown on many Chevrolet promotional and advertising photographs.

The year of the big change also prompted a change in wheel covers. A redesigned hubcap was furnished with the 500 models. A 500 full wheel cover could be ordered. The plastic insert displayed a red triangle similar to the triangle on the front panel. The Monza and Corsa had their own wheel cover marked by the plastic center insert.

This hubcap was standard equipment on the 1965 500.

A 1965 Monza wheel cover is shown above.

This 1965 wheel cover carries the Corsa insert.

In 1966 the standard hub cap design remained the same. The wheel cover center was enlarged but the emblem design remained the same.

This 1966 wheel cover illustrates the enlarged center and the 500 emblem.

The Monza insert for 1966 is highlighted in this photograph.

Note the painted accent stripes surrounding the Corsa emblem. These accent stripes were unique to the 1965 and 1966 Corsa wheel covers.

The style of the 500 hubcap changed for the last time in 1967. Our investigation turned up two hubcap designs. One sported a frosted center while the other design featured a polished center. As in previous years, wheel covers were optional for the 500 model.

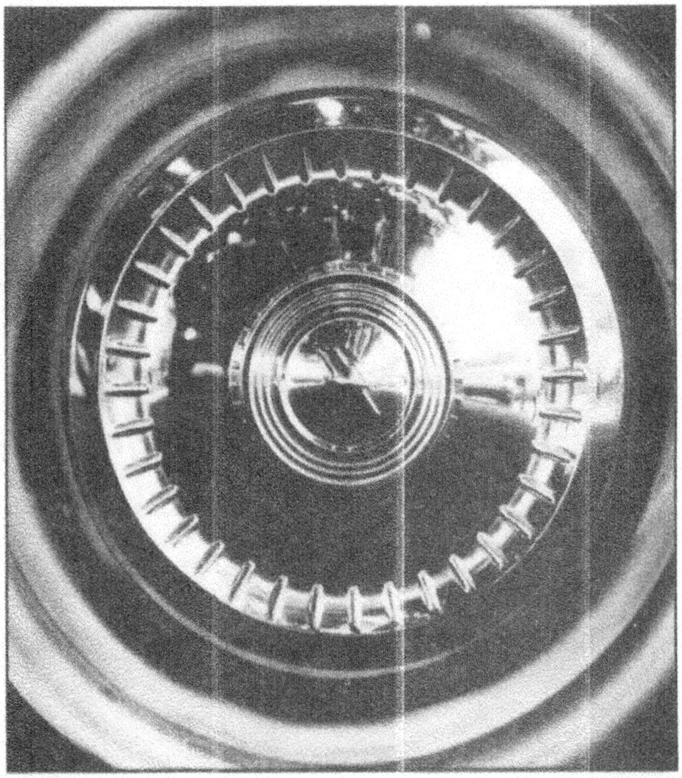

These pictures show the two 500 hubcap designs used 1967 through 1969. Above shows the polished center and the bottom picture shows the frosted center.

In 1967 the U.S. Department of Transportation outlawed knock off hubs. The simulated wire wheel covers offered that year, and through the remainder of production years, did not have knock off bars.

The spinner bars were eliminated from the last simulated wire wheel covers.

All of the other wheel cover designs carried over from 1966 and remained the same through the end of the 1969 production year.

Wheels

The various wheel cover designs can be confusing, but wheel color, which should be simple, is even more perplexing. Many thanks to Larry Claypool for his *STOCK IS* column that formed the basis for the following information.

In 1960, on the 500 and 700 models, the wheel color was the same as the body color. If the 1960 Monza was ordered from the factory with blackwall tires, the wheel color was the same as the body. If the Monza was ordered from the factory with whitewalls, the wheel color was black.

For the years 1961 through 1964 the wheel color matched the body if blackwalls were ordered from the factory. If whitewalls and hubcaps were ordered from the factory, the wheels were painted the body color. However, if whitewalls and wheel covers were ordered from the factory, the wheels were painted black.

The Monzas and Spyders for the years 1961-1964 continued the confusion. If whitewalls were ordered from the factory, the wheels were painted black. If blackwall tires were ordered from the factory the wheel color matched the body colors, even though wheel covers were standard on all Monzas and Spyders.

The second generation Corvairs cleared up the confusion slightly. On the 500 model, if the standard hubcaps were ordered, the wheel color matched the body. If the optional wheel covers were ordered for the 500, wheels were painted black. On the Monzas and Corsa models, wheel covers were standard. The wheels were always black.

Added to this complicated scheme is the fact that many dealers switched whitewalls for factory blackwall tires without changing the wheel color. Therefore, almost any wheel color, tire style, hubcap, or wheel cover combination can be rationalized.

Tires

B.F. Goodrich supplied all of General Motors original tires, so of course, supplied all of the tires for the Corvair. The early models took a 6.50 x13 inch size tire mounted on a 5.5 inch rim. According to Tony Fiore in *The Corvair Decade*, the small size wheel and tire was used to compensate for the oversteer inherent in the car. According to a Society of Automotive Engineering paper by K.H. Hansen of Chevrolet, the 6.50 x 13 inch tire on a 5.5 inch wheel developed better cornering characteristics than the 7.50 x 14 inch tires on a 5 inch rim that were used on other Chevrolet passenger cars. A set of 13 inch tires were also about 19 pounds lighter than the 14 inch tires.

From 1960 through 1964 the wheels were held on with 4 lugs. The 1965 through 1969 wheels were anchored with 5 lugs.

In 1962, the station wagon was equipped with 7.00 x 13 inch tires. In 1966 the tire size was changed to 7.00 x 13 inch on all models.

The tire designations have changed so that today the proper tire sizes would be:

6.50 x 13 = 175 x 75 or 175 x 80. Earlier replacements included B78 or 175.

7.00 x 13 = C x 78 or 185 or 185 x 75 or 185 x 80

Just a note on tire pressures. One oft raised criticism of the Corvair was the handling characteristics. The handling problems of the car were reduced when the proper tire pressures were maintained. The owners manuals recommended 15 pounds per square inch pressure for the front tires, and 26 pounds per square inch for the rear. It was recommended that the spare carry 26 psi, and if put on the front, be reduced to 15 psi. A large air pressure differential between the front and rear tires was quite unusual, and many owners who did not heed inflation instructions. Thus many Corvairs handled sluggishly and cornered poorly. Even straight line driving could prove tricky with improperly inflated tires. Cross winds increased the handling problems of cars with improperly inflated tires.

HUB CAPS AND WHEEL COVERS

1964

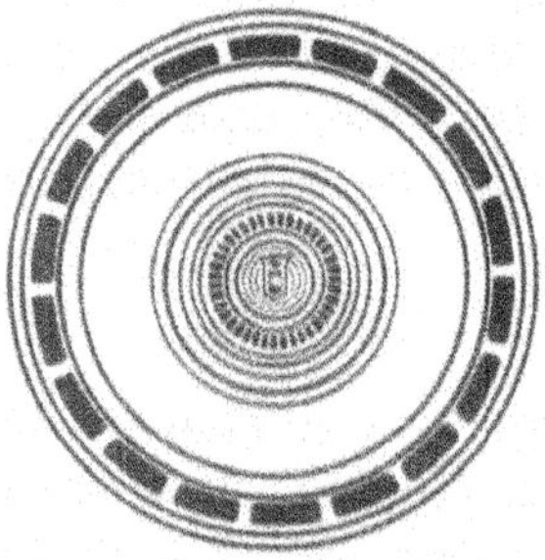

3840301*

1965

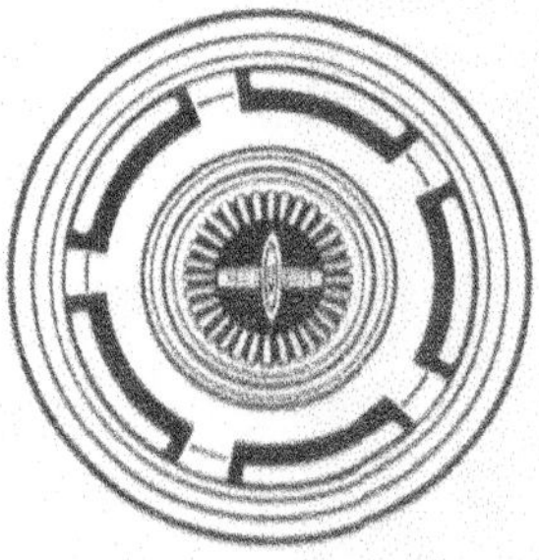

3861087*

1965-66

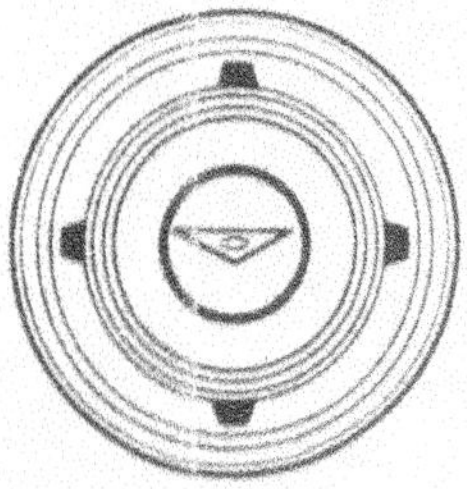

3859254

1966

3878318*

1964-66

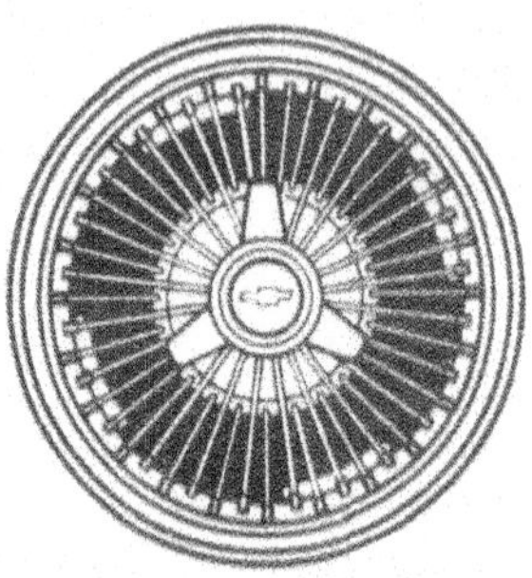

3855383-13"

3834904-14"

1965-66

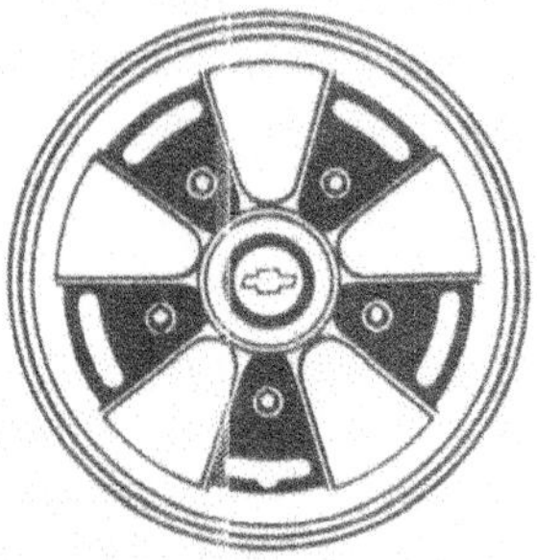

3874648-13"
986416▲

1967-69

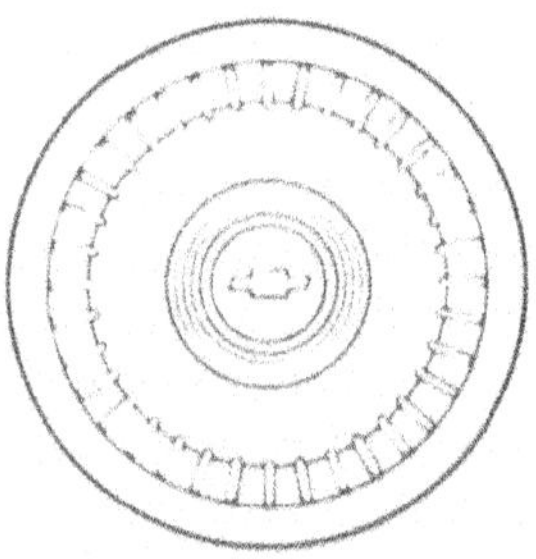

3840898
STD. ON 500 MODELS

1967-69

3878318-(1)*

1967-69

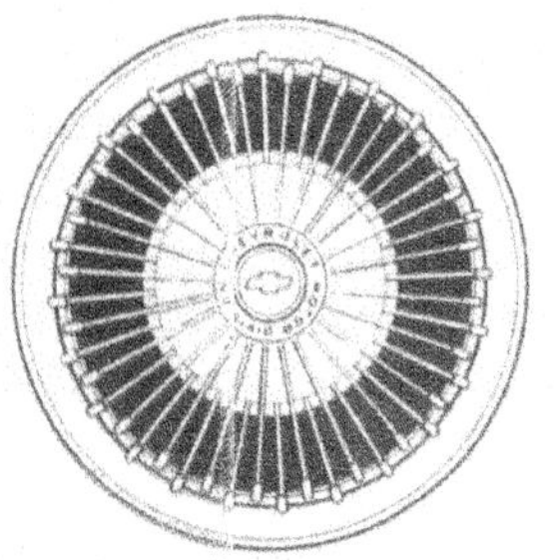

3908393
OPT. ON ALL MODELS
W/13" WHEEL

* – LESS INSERT
▲ – CONSISTS OF 4 WHEEL COVERS

Chapter 5

Interior

Dashboard

In 1960, the dashboard on the bottom of the line 500 model was very plain. It came only in a mouse gray color.

Both the 700 model and the Monza had a painted dash that matched the color of the painted metal on the doors. Non-glare paint was used on the dash and this gave a darker hue than the door paint. The 1960 through 1964 models with white upholstery used red trim on the dash. The 1962 gold upholstery used a green or olive drab trim color, and in 1963 the saddle upholstery was accented with a dark brown dash. Prior to 1963 the light blue upholstery was complimented with a matching dash. In 1963 and 1964, a darker blue dash was standard with the light blue upholstery.

In 1965 there was only one exception to the dash color not matching the interior color. If a Monza or Corsa coupe was ordered with white interior, a black or aqua dash could be provided. If a four door Monza or Corsa with a white interior was ordered, only an aqua dash was offered.

A padded dash was offered on all models as a factory installed option through the 1965 production year. Starting with the 1966 model year, safety requirements mandated by the government required padding on the dashboard of all cars sold in America.

A major change in the dashboard shape and appearance was made in 1967. Safety requirements mandated thicker padding that extended around the edges of the dashboard.

Safety considerations prompted additional padding in 1968. The noticeably thicker dash padding extended around the radio and even the ash tray. The windshield pillars were padded for the first time. This padding was carried forward to the 1969 model.

Glove Box

Although the size and basic shape of the dashboard remained the same from 1960 until 1965, the glove box door design changed. The glove box door of the 1960 and 1961 500 model was painted a lighter shade of gray than the dash, but was devoid of decoration. The radio trim was the same as the glove box door.

The glove box door on the 1960 and 1961 basic 500 models was very plain in keeping with the stark dashboard.

The glove box doors of the 1960 and 1961 700 models were faced with anodized aluminum and carried identical 700 designations.

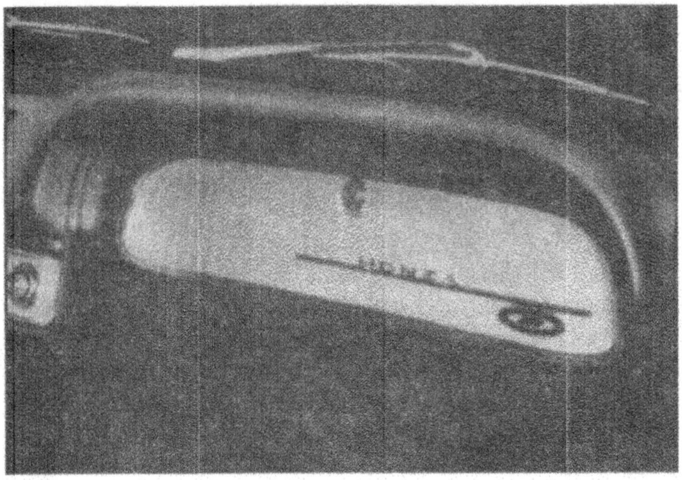

The 1960 Monza featured the same "screen door pattern" and anodized aluminum face as the 700 model, but featured a 900 logo.

The design on the glove box door was changed to a bright checkerboard pattern on the 1962 Monza.

In 1963, the pattern on the glove box door was changed to a series of horizontal bars. The glove box door and the radio bezel of the Monza Spyder had a smooth satin finish. The glove box door carried the Monza and Spyder logos.

The 1963 Monza glove box door had a bold horizontal pattern.

The next year, 1964, bright metal corrugated verticality, faced the glove box door on all models except the Spyder. A smooth satin finish highlighted the Spyder glove box door. Only the Spyder logo was placed on the glove box door in 1964.

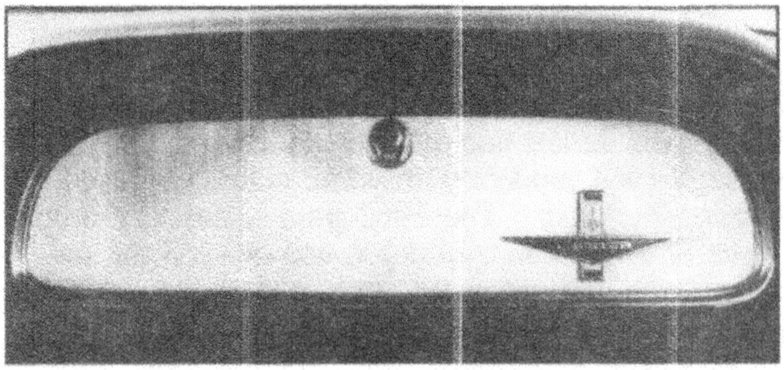

The pattern on the glove box door changed in 1964, but the logo remained the same.

The glove box door and surrounding panel on the 1965 500 model was painted the same color as the dashboard. The door was devoid of decoration.

The finish on the glove box door and surrounding panel in the Monza and Corsa models matched the instrument panel cutout. Both areas featured a coarse matte or crinkle finish. The Monza glove box door featured a light color while the Corsa door was done in black. Both models featured a thin aluminum accent strip. The model emblem was located in the upper right portion of the door. The remainder of the dash was done in a pleasing contrasting color.

The next year, 1966, the black coarse matte finish was used on both the Monza and Corsa models. The 500 dash was painted to match the interior upholstery. A lock became a standard feature on the glove box door on all models.

The 1965 Monza glove box (above) had a light finish. The 1966 Monza glove box (below) sported the same dark matte finish that the Corsa used both years.

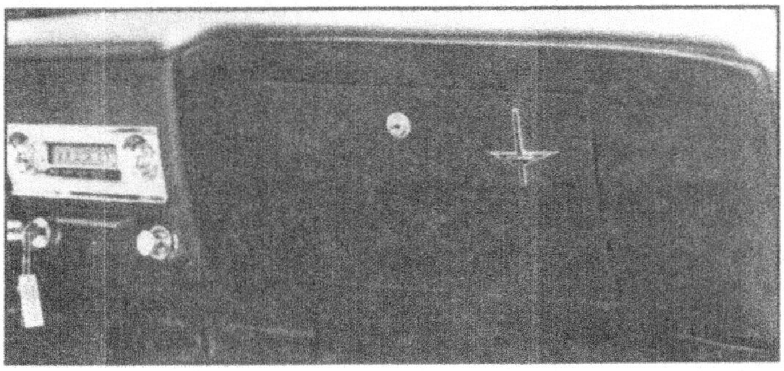

Instrument Cluster

The instrument cluster in 1960 was pure basics with few frills in design or style. The only gauges were for gasoline level and the speedometer/odometer. Separate red oil pressure and overheating lights took care of the rest of the engine functions. Green directional signal arrows were placed to the outside of the two gauges. A red bright light indicator was centered under the 50 mile per hour designation on the speedometer.

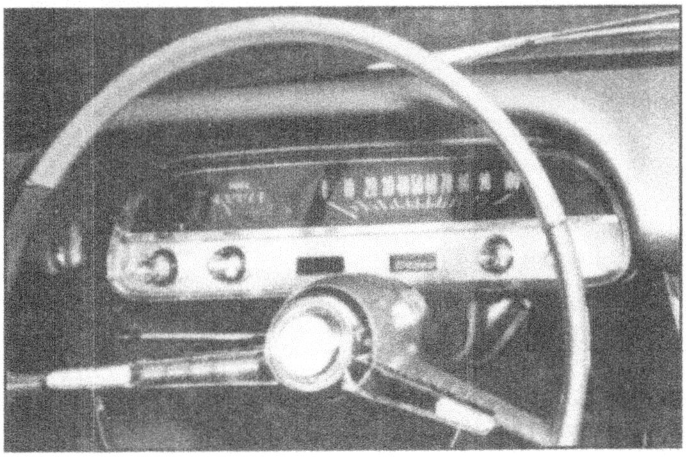

The first generation Corvairs had an uncluttered instrument panel.

The instrument panel bezel on the 500 models was painted gray. An anodized aluminum bezel with chrome trim was featured on the 700 and Monza series. The pattern on the instrument panel bezel changed each year and was the same as the pattern on the glove box door.

A key switch, a three position light switch, wiper controls, and a cigarette lighter were positioned in a line below the gauges and function lights. The cigarette lighter was an option until 1962, so if not ordered in 1960 or 1961, a bright metal plug filled the hole in the dash.

The control knob functions were embossed in the bezel trim. This knob design was used only one year.

The 1960 oil pressure light label proclaimed "OIL ENG" above the idiot light. In 1961 the label was changed to "ENGINE". The label for a manual choke was added to the instrument panel bezel between the wiper and oil pressure gauge labels. The choke control itself was hung below the dash, appearing as an add on. The manual choke was dropped after 1961.

Close inspection will reveal that these 1961 knobs are different than the 1960 knobs. This design was used through 1964. Although the choke knob is missing, the support is evident below the dash.

The 1962, 1963 and 1964, Spyder models had a unique instrument cluster that set this model off as a true "sports car". Rather than the rectangular gauges featured in other Corvairs, the Spyder had round dials and indicator lights.

The gauge needles were white in 1962. These were changed to red for the 1963 and 1964 models, adding almost imperceptively to the sporting image.

The tachometer and speedometer dominated the instrument cluster. The tachometer was on the far left and the speedometer centered. The speedometer included both an odometer and a trip odometer. The light switch was located in the lower left corner of the instrument panel. The small left turn indicator light was above the light switch. The red bright light indicator was centered below the tach and speedometer.

Grouped to the right of the speedometer in a triangular cluster were the manifold pressure gauge (upper left), the head temperature gauge (upper right) and the fuel gauge (centered below). The twin red warning lights for the generator / fan and the temperature / pressure were located to the left of the fuel gauge. Balancing them on the right of the fuel gauge was the ignition key switch. The right turn indicator lamp, located in the upper right hand corner of the panel, completed the instrumentation. The cigarette lighter and the wiper switch were mounted on a separate plate below the red bright light indicator.

In 1965, the instrument panel bore no resemblance to earlier models. Three circular and deeply recessed instruments dominated the panel. Flanking an optional clock were a fuel gauge to the right and a speedometer to the left. The engine function warning lights for oil pressure, and for the generator / fan belt, were located in a half circle below the fuel gauge. In 1967 a brake warning light was added to the instrument cluster. It was positioned between the existing two lights on the gas gauge. This light warned the driver if one of the two brake master cylinders was malfunctioning or if the hand brake was engaged.

The lights and windshield wiper on-off switch were to the left of the speedometer. The heater controls were relocated to the right of the gas gauge on the lower edge of the dashboard. The automatic transmission shift lever was above the heat controls. The two green turn signal lights were nestled below and on either side of the clock.

This dash design was used for both the 500 and Monza from 1965 through 1969. The knob design was used in 1965 and 1966.

Corsa, the top of the line model, featured an instrument cluster more reminiscent of a sports car than the early Corvairs. The fully recessed circular gauges were clustered directly in front of the driver.

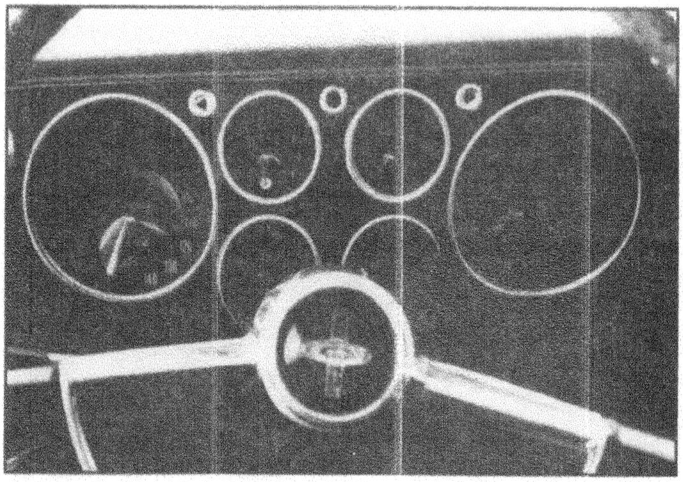

The Corsa used this sporty appearing instrument cluster for the two years of production.

A large speedometer to the left included a trip odometer. Centered at the six o'clock position was a generator / fan indicator light. Immediately to the right of the speedometer, a four cluster group of instruments were recessed in smaller housings. Top left was a clock, top right a cylinder head temperature gauge, bottom right a manifold pressure gauge and bottom left a fuel gauge. A tachometer was housed to the right of this cluster in a recess matching the speedometer. The turn signal lights and high beam indicator light were spaced between the clock and head temperature gauge. Heater controls were located directly below the tachometer.

Radio

The radio was a factory or dealer installed option for all years. The first generation Corvairs had no built in space for the radio. It was mounted below the dash between the instrument cluster and the glove box. The the radio speaker grille was located in the top center of the dashboard behind the ashtray.

In 1960 a manually operated AM radio was the only receiver offered.

This radio was found in a 1961 700. It was reported to be rare because of the letters on the buttons.

This pushbutton radio was installed in a 1962 Monza.

In 1963, full transistor radios were introduced. That same year and in 1964, rear speakers were offered as an extra with the push button radios on all models except the convertibles. Push button radios were available on convertibles, but rear seat speakers were not. The rear speaker was centered in the small shelf behind the back seat. The manually operated sets were still available.

The later models, those after 1964, had a space in the dash for the radio. When no radio was installed, a cover was placed over the opening. The cover was painted the color of the dash but had a bright aluminum trim piece. Since the ignition switch and lighter were mounted below the radio opening, the cover plate was embossed with "ACC OFF ON START" and "LIGHTER". When a radio was installed, the radio trim plate carried the same legend.

Note the trim piece below the radio plate embossed with the key and lighter functions.

In 1965, the options for radios were the manual, the push-button, and the AM/FM push-button sets. The front speaker was mounted below the two center grilles in the top of the dash.

This 1965 model was one of the last manual radios offered.

Optional rear speakers were available when selecting a push-button set. The rear speakers were not available on convertibles.

In 1966, according to Fiore, or 1967 according to Claypool, the manually operated radio was discontinued. A standard AM radio and an AM/FM model, both with push-button tuning, were offered.

In 1969 the dashboard padding mandated by safety regulations almost engulfed the push button radio.

In 1965 an AM/FM multiplex system was offered as optional equipment. This system was similar to those in bigger cars and included four separate speakers. The multiplex system included front/rear and left/right controls. We never found this option listed on the factory options list, nor did we run across any installations in the cars we saw.

Auxiliary speakers were offered on all models in 1966. The speakers we observed were mounted on the passenger side below the small shelf behind the rear seat. This allowed the optional rear window defroster to be mounted under the center of the shelf. These options continued through 1967, 1968, and 1969.

Ash Tray

The ash tray for the driver and front seat passengers was mounted in the dashboard. From 1960 through 1964, it was on top of the dash, centered between the instrument cluster and the glove box. The cover slid toward the windshield when opened.

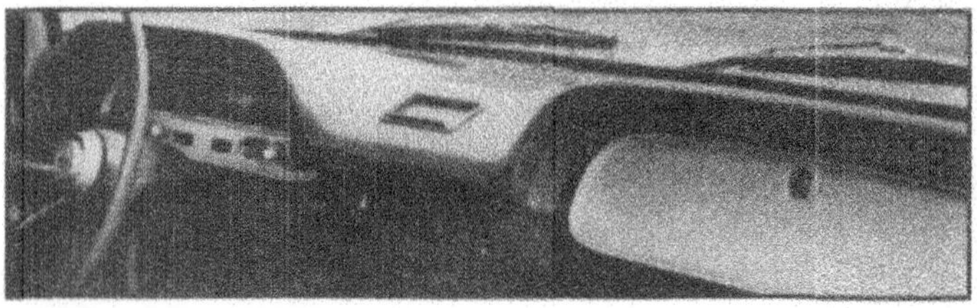

The ash tray cover was painted the color of the dashboard.

On the 1965 through 1969 models the ash tray was located below the radio space between the ignition switch and the lighter. The door pulled down to open.

On the late models, the ash tray was again painted the same color as the dash. Note the large handle. on this 1966 Corsa

In 1965, a full length lip served as the handle. In 1966, a larger handle was added. The final design change in 1968 incorporated a recess in the padding beneath the ash tray. The recess provided easier access to the cover.

Safety padding required a major change in ash tray design. The manual radio in this 1969 500 is not stock equipment for that year.

Air Conditioner

No air-conditioning unit was offered in 1960. From 1961 until 1964, it was available as a dealer or factory installed option on all sedans and coupes. Air-conditioners were not available on the Spyder models or station wagon models. Information suggests that it was available on only models equipped with a radio.

The air conditioner was suspended from the center of the dash below the radio. A rectangular vent was mounted on the face of the cool air distributor. There was a round vent on either side of the unit that directed air toward the floor.

The chromed controls were on either side of the rectangular center vent. The blower control was on the left. The blower had three speeds, low, medium, and high.

Two round vents, not apparent in the photograph, were located on the sides of the unit. Note the Corvair name plate.

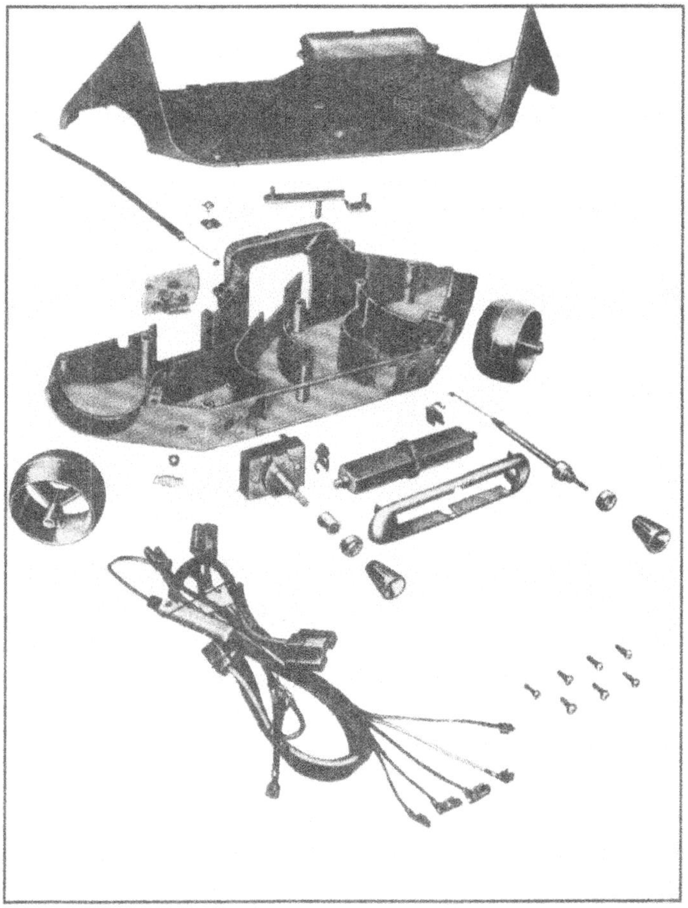

Drawing 9-3 in the Chassis and Body Parts Catalog (Nov. 1976) details the 1961 through 1964 air conditioning distributor.

From 1965 until 1969, an air conditioner was again offered as optional equipment. The air conditioner was a factory option only. Different controls were used to operate the heater, defroster and air conditioner. A fourth control switch was added. The fan switch was relocated to the top of the control unit.

The rectangular dash vents with exposed baffles directed the cool air. A round vent was located on each side of the dash close to the doors. These vents were fed by hoses running from a distributor behind the center of the dash. A blower was mounted in the luggage compartment. The compressor and condenser were in the engine compartment. The radio mounted below the center air conditioning vent.

The air conditioner controls are visible to the left of the key switch.

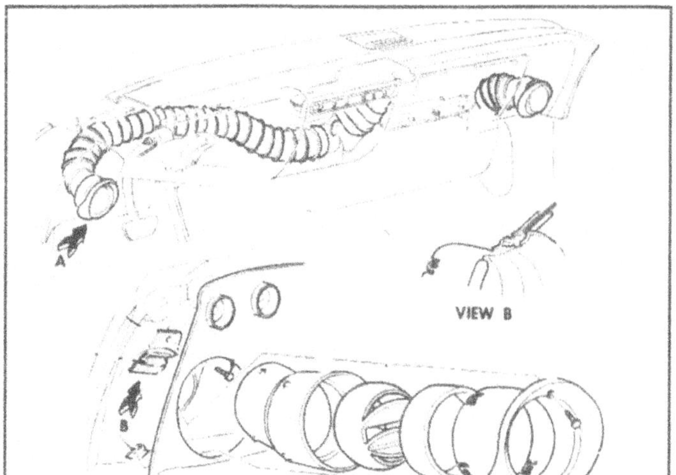

Drawing 9-5 in the Chassis and Body Parts Catalog (Nov. 1976) details the 1965 through 1969 air conditioner distribution system.

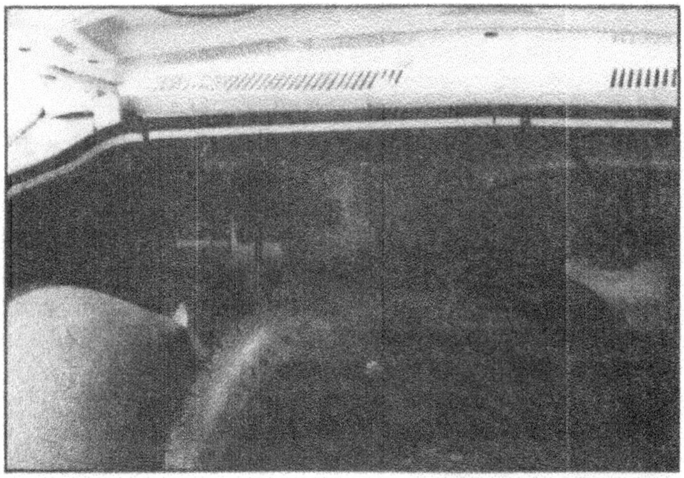

The air conditioner blower unit was located in the luggage compartment of second generation Corvairs.

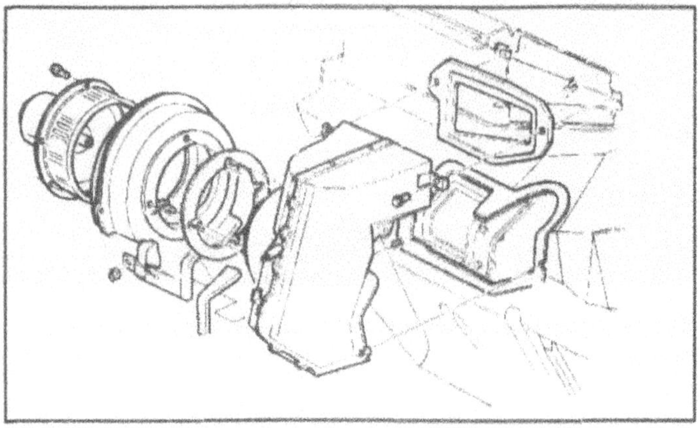

Drawing 9-4 in the Chassis and Body Parts Catalog (Nov. 1976) details the 1965 through 1969 air conditioner blower and air inlet.

Heater and Defroster

A gasoline heater and defroster were options offered on the first Corvairs in 1960. The heater and blower were located on the passenger's side in the front luggage compartment. The location of the heater was a major reason that luggage space was at a premium. Many people appreciated the fast warm up feature of the gas heater, but it certainly had drawbacks. Owners falsely thought that it would guzzle gas, malfunctions often caused scary noises and smoke, and no doubt the direct air heater was cheaper to produce.

In 1961 the gas heater was replaced with a forced air system that used the engine heat. The gas heater remained as standard equipment on the trucks and as an option on the automobiles until 1962, when it was phased out completely.

In the forced air system, outside air was passed over the engine, collected and heated in a shroud and directed through flexible tubes to the interior ducts.

Warm air was delivered to the front seat passengers through vents under each door. Warm air was routed through the hose behind the door frame to the twin defroster vents in the top of the dash.

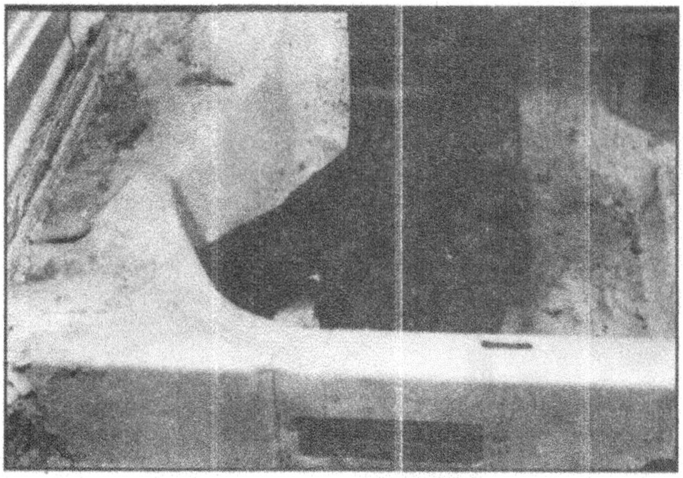

The rear seat passengers were warmed from dual vents located under the rear seats. The photograph shows the right (passenger side) rear seat duct.

The windshield was defrosted from twin vents in the top of the dash. The warm air was routed from the floor vents to the dash through a flexible hose.

The controls for the heater and defroster were located on the lower edge of the dash between the radio (if so equipped) and the steering column. The three speed fan switch was off when to the far left and on high when switched to the far right. The black plastic knobs beneath the fan switch controlled the air flow. The one on the far left regulated the heat, the middle one the air, and the right hand knob operated the defroster.

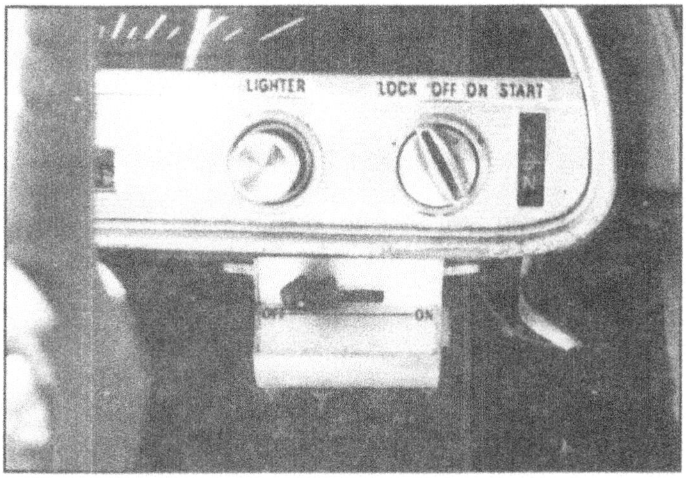

The control unit was the same for the gas heater and the forced air system.

The heat distribution system in the restyled second generation Corvair was redesigned. Once again air was warmed in the manifold shroud. An electric blower moved the warm air through the collecting ducts and into the tunnel under the floor. A single vent off the tunnel supplied warm air to the rear seat passengers. Front seat passengers were warmed by air from a single vent located under the dash.

The single front heater vent on the late model Corvairs was located on the heater tunnel.

Heat ducts from the center tunnel to dashboard vents directed hot defrosting air to the windshield. Four grilles were cut in the top of the dash. The two outside grilles measured 5 inches x 3.75 inches and contained 12 fins. Hot air passed through these grilles to defrost the windshield. The two inside grilles measured 4.25 inches x 3.75 inches and were for the radio speakers.

In 1968 a forced air rear window defroster was added to the list of optional equipment. This, of course, was not available on the convertibles.

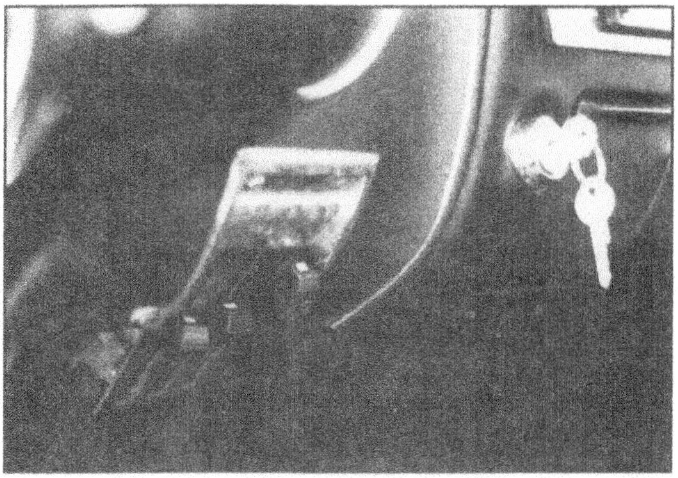

Heating and defrosting were controlled by three knobs to the left of the key switch. The defroster control was on the right, the heat control center, and the fan switch on the left.

Fresh Air Ventilation System

A fresh air ventilation system was available on all Corvairs. The air intake was through the front cowl. Fresh air was delivered through a vent below the dash in the sidewall, just forward of the front doors. Each vent operated independently with a pull knob.

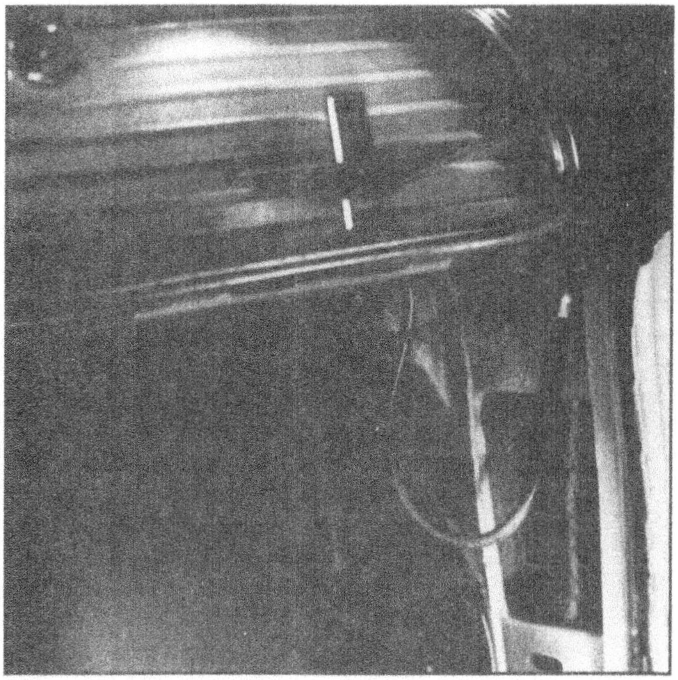

Note the fresh air vent opening in the lower center of this picture. The plastic grille has been removed.

Changes to the fresh air ventilation system were made in 1965. The plastic grille covering the vent opening was enlarged. Newly styled knobs were housed in a recess in the sidewall.

The 1965 enlargement of the fresh air vent and recessed control knob are evident on this Monza.

Steering Column

An innovative telescoping steering column was introduced as a 1965 option. The center of the steering wheel acted as a locking device and the steering column could be lengthened or shortened three inches with a slight tug or push on the wheel. The telescoping steering column continued to be offered through the 1969 model year.

After the telescoping steering column was adjusted to the most comfortable position, the driver simply tightened down the center hub. Note the flanges on the hub.

As a safety feature, an energy absorbing steering column was offered as an option in 1966. A special coupling and plate in the column absorbed some of the impact from a collision.

An all new collapsible steering column assembly was introduced in 1967. This column was optional equipment for all models through the 1969 model year.

Steering Wheel

The "plain Jane" Corvairs that rolled off the assembly line in 1960 were steered with a wheel exactly in keeping with the car's character. The closest they came to "fancy" was the finger grip contours on the windshield side. The color of the wheel matched the interior color. The horn button was placed in the center of the column. The button displayed a large "C" surrounding the letters "orvair". In addition there was a "stylized arrow or a wheat head" decoration.

The gray 500 wheel, made of a plastic composition material, had two spokes. The color of the 700 steering wheel (above) matched the interior and carried the same emblem as the 500 and Monza.

The Monza featured a deluxe steering wheel with a chrome plated horn ring and center button. The plastic center of the button displayed the same emblem as the 500 and 700 models.

The 1960 Monza wheel was two tone in color with bright metal bands separating the colors.

The horn button design was the same in 1960 and 1961.

The basic 1961 steering wheel remained the same as in 1960. The deluxe steering wheel and horn ring, standard equipment on the Monza, were optional equipment items for the 500 and 700 series.

In 1962, the steering wheel design did not change. The 500 and 700 model continued to be very plain, while the Monza models sported a wheel with chrome trim and horn ring. This deluxe wheel could be ordered as optional equipment on the 500 and 700 series.

Close inspection of the steering wheel pictures reveals a slight change in the horn ring of the Monza between 1960 and 1962. The thumb pads on the 1962 and 1963 Monza horn ring (above) are smaller than those on the 1960 ring. We could not document which year this change took place.

The changes on this 1964 Monza steering wheel are in the horn ring, and center emblem.

The horn button changed several times between 1960 and 1964. We examined a stock 1964 Spyder. The horn button carried the Monza logo. We were told that other Spyders used the Spyder emblem. Horn buttons may have been a running change.

This horn button was on a 1963 Monza Spyder.

Monza horn buttons 1963 through 1969 are pictured above. Left to right: 1963; 1964; 1965; 1966 through 1969.

While the 1965 500 continued to have a very plain steering wheel, the other models were changed. The standard equipment steering wheel for the Monza and Corsa models was a two spoke, two tone wheel. The wheel was dished out to accept the horn ring. The half circle horn ring did not have the split bar supports.

An austere steering wheel followed the 500 model through major design changes.

The Monza retained the two toned steering wheel despite many major design changes in the rest of the car.

The horn ring on the Monza and Corsa was identical. The center logo was used to distinguish between the models.

A sport styled steering wheel with the horn button in the hub was offered as an option. This plastic steering wheel featured a simulated wood grain pattern. The hub of the steering wheels we saw were decorated with a bow tie logo.

The same steering wheels, including the simulated walnut wood grain sport wheel, were offered for 1966.

The steering wheel for the 1967 Corvair was changed from a two spoke to a three spoke design. This was done to meet federal safety standards more than for style. The three spoke design was used on all the models until production ended. A three spoked simulated wood grain steering wheel, similar to the wheel offered in 1966, was offered as optional equipment in 1967.

This 1969 500 steering wheel is the three spoke design used from 1967 through 1969.

As production wound down in 1968, the only change to the steering wheel was the trim. The trim surface was changed from a bright chrome plated to a brushed finish. The Monza steering wheel and the telescopic column were offered in 1968. The steering wheels and columns used in the 1969 models were identical to the ones used in 1968.

The horn buttons are located in the spokes of this late model Monza steering wheel.

Sun Visors

The driver's side sun visor was standard on all models for all years. The Monza was the only model mounting a right hand (passenger) sun visor for 1960. The right hand sun visor was offered as an option on the 500 and 700 models as part of the "De Luxe Body Group". The group also included arm rests and a cigarette lighter. The package was a bargain at only $11.00. Throughout the production years, the sun visors were finished in the same fabric as the headliner.

An optional passenger side sun visor on the 500 and 700 series carried through the 1961 model year. By 1962, however, when the Corvair completed it's transition from economy car to sports car, dual sun visors became standard equipment on all models.

In 1965, padded sun visors were introduced as an optional equipment item. The sun visors on the 500 were vinyl covered for the first time in 1965.

Inside Mirror

The back of the standard equipment rear view mirror for 1960 and 1961, 500 and 700 models was painted gray. The mirror was centered on the windshield and was suspended on a slim post that was anchored to the roof and window molding with three screws. The mirror was fastened to the post with a screw that allowed it to swivel.

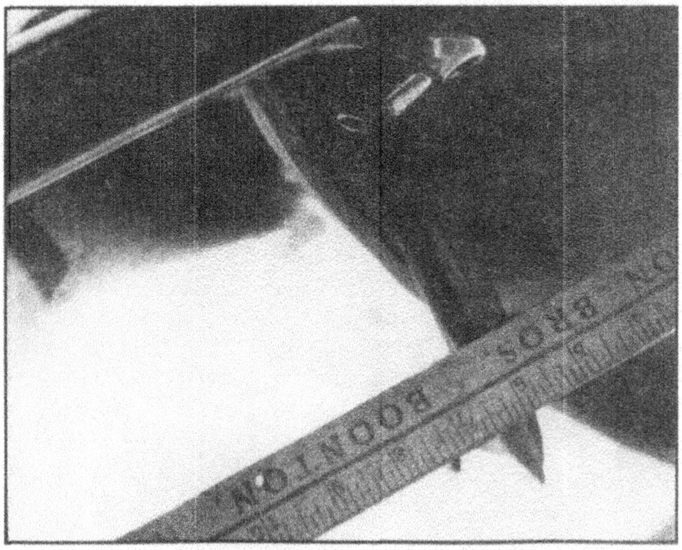

In 1966 padded visors were standard equipment on all models. Note the visor pivot assembly (below).

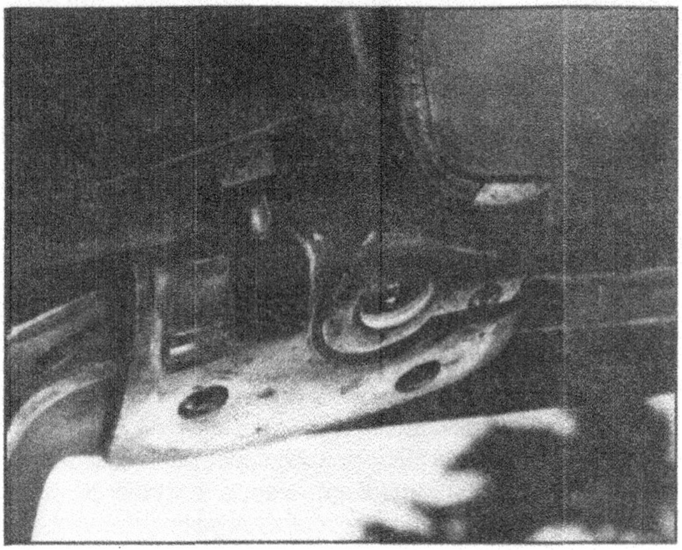

A chrome plated rear view mirror with the day/night adjustment was offered as standard equipment on the Monza and Corsa models in 1965. The mirror on the 500 model sported a brushed metal back but did not have the day/night feature. We found chrome backed mirrors on 1968 and 1969 500 models.

The mirror for the late model convertibles was mounted with three screws through a plate to the windshield top rail. This plate also secured the sun visors.

The basic mirror did not have the day/night feature.

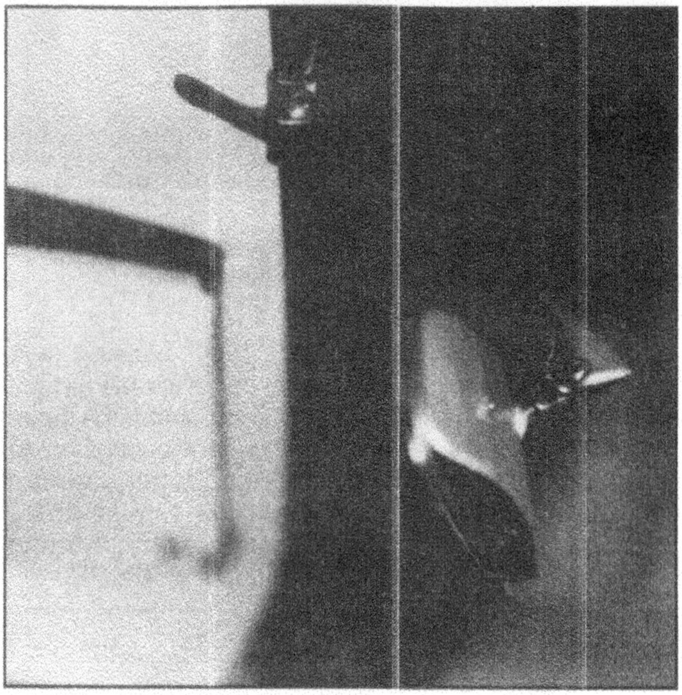

A chrome backed mirror with the day/night feature was offered as a option for all models in 1962.

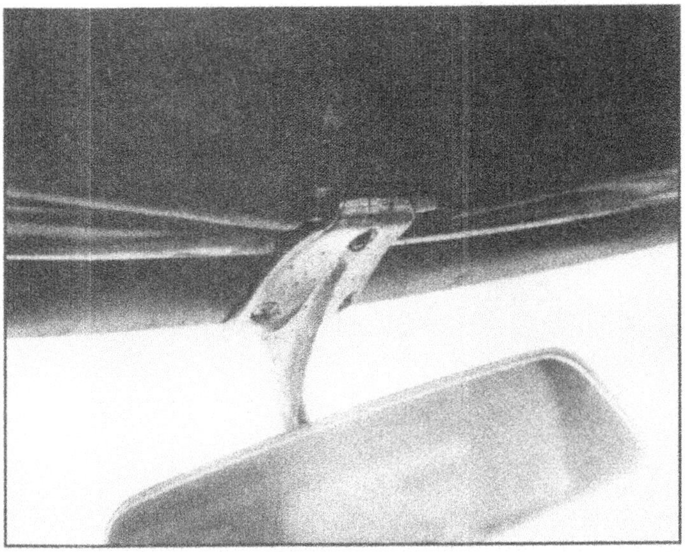

The base of the rear view mirror served as a visor anchor on the late model convertibles.

Seats

The upholstery color and fabric and interior color options are listed in chapter 6. This section will cover the general changes in the fabric and the seats. Door panels and headliner are described in following sections.

Since the Corvair was originally conceived as an economy car, the first upholstery schemes were rather modest. The original 500 model had a lightly patterned gray cloth.

The first 500 two door model had a split bench front seat.

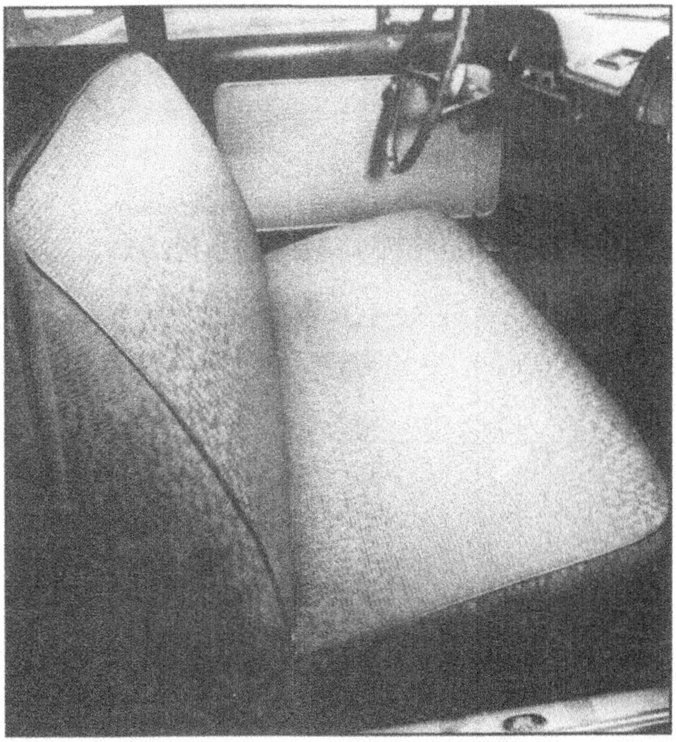

The 1960 four door 500 had a full length bench seat making it a six passenger car.

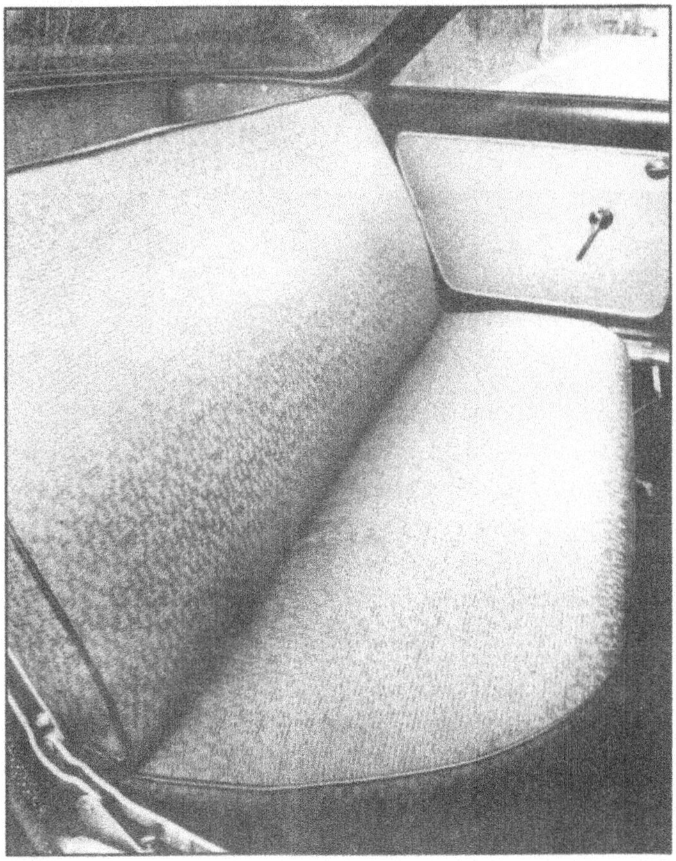

The rear seat of the 1960 500 was a full width bench seat.

The 1960 700 series offered only limited upholstery refinements. The fabric was a combination of cloth and vinyl available in three colors. The colors were keyed to the exterior paint.

The split front bench seat of the 1960 700 two door is pictured above. The full length front bench seat of the 1960 700 four door is shown below.

The rear seat of the 1960 700 was a full length, fold down, bench style.

The late arriving Monza was dressed in leather grained vinyl with a loop pile carpet on the floor. It offered front bucket seats and a rear bench seat. Chrome trimmed hinge covers on the front seats of the Monza set that model off nicely

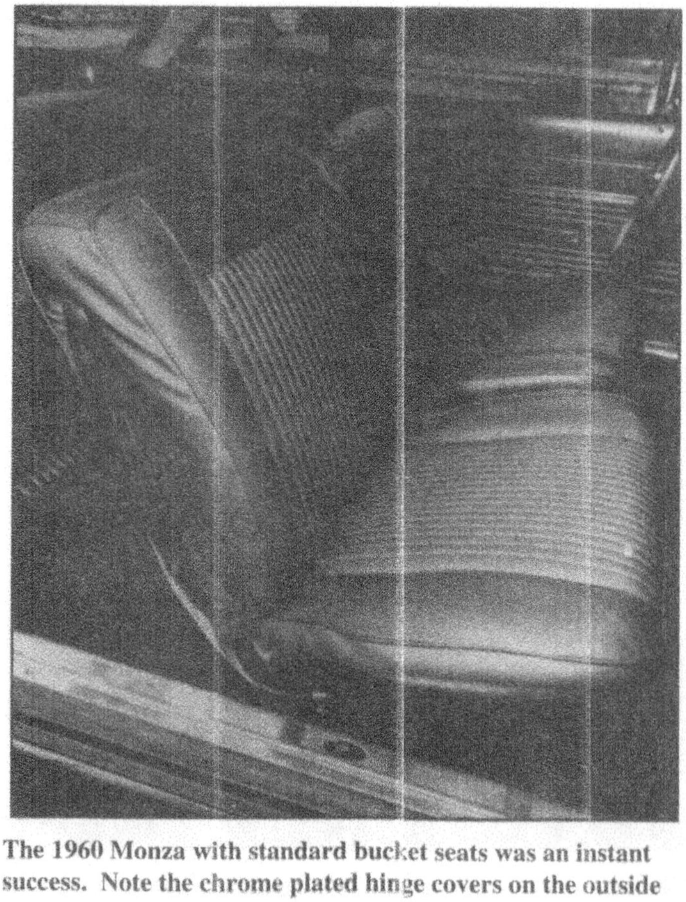

The 1960 Monza with standard bucket seats was an instant success. Note the chrome plated hinge covers on the outside hinges.

Class had its limits. Note the painted inside hinge of this 1960 Monza two door coupe.

The rear seat of the 1960 Monza was an all vinyl full length bench style. The fold down feature was standard on this model.

Bench seats remained standard equipment for the 500 and 700 series in 1961. Bucket seats were not an option. The upholstery of the 500 series was improved. It was available with the same three interior color options as the 1960 700 series.

The seat fabric of the 700 series was once again a combination of cloth and vinyl. Red was added to the color selection.

On the 1960 and 1961 700 series, a vinyl strip at the top of the seat reduced the absorption of hair oil.

The upholstery of the hot selling Monza was changed little for 1961. It was all vinyl on the coupe and a combination of good quality cloth and vinyl on the sedan models.

Sharp looking vinyl leather upholstery with vertical creases and small bright metal buttons set off the Monza two door models. Bench seats with a cloth and vinyl fabric were standard in the Monza sedan. The sedan could be ordered with front bucket seats with vinyl upholstery.

The 1962, Corvair completed the transition from "economy car" to "sport model". The color choices were changed for 1962 when the 500 and 700 models were both upgraded in fabric quality. The Monza continued to be the class of the line with the Spyder option unabashedly catering to the sports car enthusiast.

The 500 station wagon was discontinued in 1962. The 700 and Monza wagons offered all of the interior refinements of the individual series.

For 1962, the interior of the 500 series was improved by adding combination cloth and vinyl fabric. The new checked design came in three colors. Most owners felt the vinyl door panels were far more attractive than the previous ones.

The quality of the seat upholstery was correspondingly upgraded on the 700 series. The pattern of the upholstery also underwent a major change. A vertical vinyl "ladder" was embossed in the center of the bench seat. It gave the illusion of separated bucket seats. The cloth on either side of the vinyl sported a checkered pattern.

Although there were pattern changes in the seat coverings on the Monza models in 1962, the upholstery combinations of cloth and vinyl fabric remained the same as in 1961.

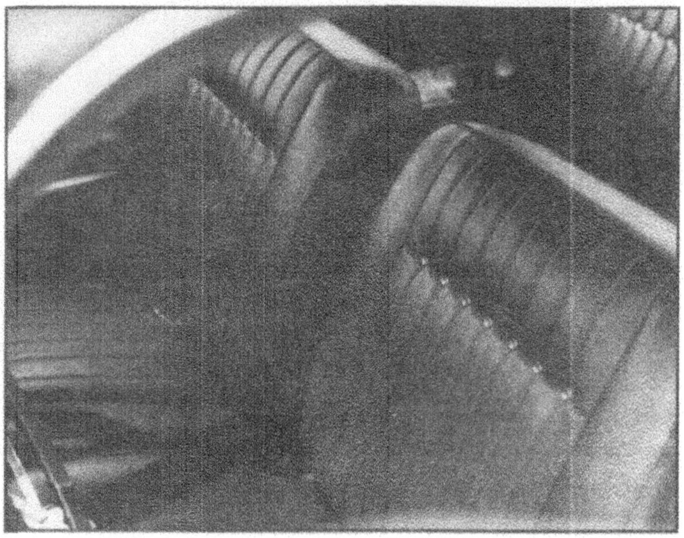

The vinyl upholstery of the 1962 Monza was set off with a row of small bright buttons.

In 1963, the 500 and 700 series had upholstery that was similar in quality to 1962, but offered new patterns and colors. Clearly the emphasis had been put on the Monza and Monza Spyder models for 1963. The Monza and Monza Spyder continued to sell well due, in no small part, to the craftsmanship that went into the interiors.

A new seat upholstery design, which featured rectangular decorator buttons, set off the 1963 Monza and Spyder models.

By 1964, the 500 Corvair came only in a coupe model. As usual the upholstery was less desirable than the 700 model. The 700 now came only in a four door sedan and had a vinyl and cloth upholstery in a slightly different pattern than the previous year.

The Spyder became a separate series in 1964 and was the top of the Corvair line. High quality vinyl upholstery continued to be a feature of the Monza and Spyder models. The pattern of the upholstery changed to a rectangular motif, but the fabric, colors and options remained as they were in 1963.

The Monza and Spyder now came with front bucket seats as standard equipment.

The upholstery of the 1965 Corvair underwent a massive styling change. The 500 series, which now came in two door and four door sedan models, was still the bottom of the line. The upholstery offered was all vinyl for the first time. A bench seat in front and back made the 1965 500 the only six passenger car in the Corvair line. The upholstery came in a choice of three colors keyed to the exterior color. The upholstery pattern was alternating basket weave and smooth vinyl.

The upholstery of the restyled Monza continued to be of durable vinyl. The newly introduced Corsa model carried the same high quality upholstery as the Monza.

The front bucket seats of the 1965 Monza and Corsa models were standard equipment. They were covered with premium vinyl leather. Vertical pleats were the dominant pattern. The rear fold down, bench style seat carried the same pattern.

Headrests for the front seats first became available as factory options in 1966. Pictures of this option are rare. We were advised that the headrest was supported by two chrome finished rods fastened to the exterior of the seat back. The rods were adjustable and fastened with thumb screws.

Note the absence of decorative buttons and the chrome plated inside hinge on this 1965 Corsa front seat.

In 1967, the Monza offered new, slimmer bucket seats. These were referred to as the "astro" design in Chevrolet literature. The upholstery was unchanged for the 1967 model year and mirrors the 1966 model in material and design. Headrests were still offered as options.

The all vinyl upholstery offered on the 1966 500 series had a similar pattern, but was of better quality than the fabric used the previous year.

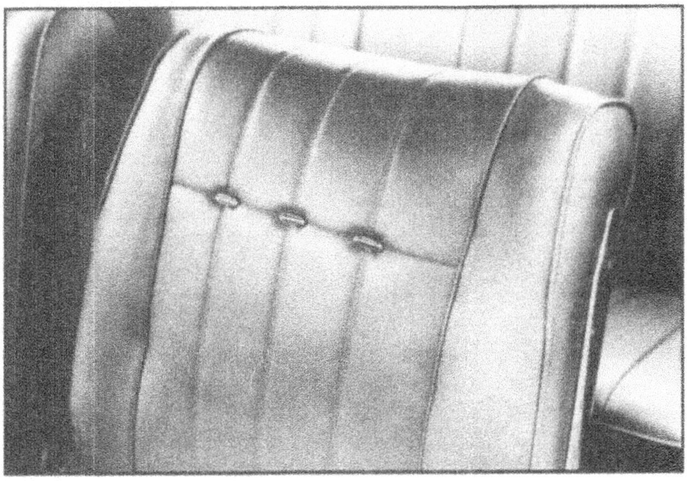

In 1968, the design of the upholstery changed for the last time. The quality of the vinyl was poor compared to previous years. Some references list it as vinyl coated fabric and not vinyl leather. This poor quality material continued to be a complaint against the 1968 and 1969 models 20 years later.

The new "astro" seats were a big change in a year that saw few changes in the Corvair.

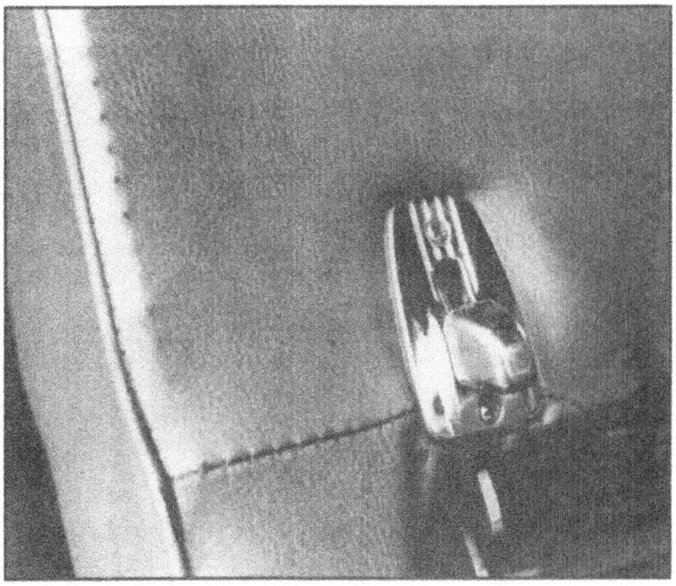

The front seats of two door models were now equipped with a latch to prevent accidental folding.

(left)
The pattern of the seat upholstery for the 1966 Monza and Corsa models was changed to a ribbed design set off by three bright metal buttons. Note the painted hinge on this Monza.

In 1968, the 500 model featured bench seats with a lightly patterned vinyl fabric separated by a smooth section in the middle. The Monza series seats had four horizontal pleats on the seat, and three on the back rest. The pleats on the back rest were set off with small rectangular trim buttons. For the sake of safety, the backs of the bucket seats on the Monza models, previously painted metal, were now made of an impact absorbing plastic material.

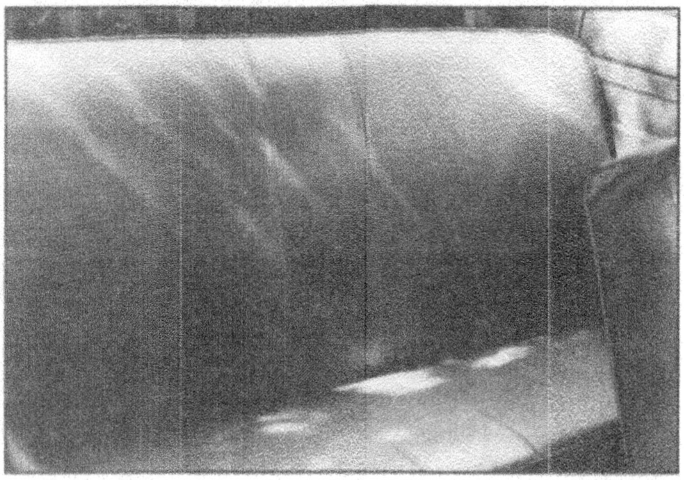

The upholstery pattern in this 1969 500 model was identical to the pattern used in 1968.

Head rests were mandatory for the first and last time on the 1969 Corvair. The Monza upholstery pattern carried over from 1968.

Fold Down Rear Seat Back

The fold down rear seat back was a very useful Corvair innovation. It increased cargo space and blunted a common criticism from those customers changing from a larger car to a smaller car. The 500 and 700 series may have suffered in sales because it was not standard equipment. The fold down seat back was an option for those models through 1964. The seat was never offered for the first generation convertible body style, but was standard equipment on the Monza two and four door models.

These two photographs show the fold down rear seat back on a 1961 700 model. This design created a small storage area behind the seat back (above). The seat was anchored with a scissor hinge on each side (below).

In 1965, the folding rear seat back was standard equipment on the Monza and Corsa models. It remained an optional item on the 500 model Corvair through 1969. If four door models equipped with the fold down rear seat back also had rear arm rests, the rear doors had to be opened so the seat back could be folded down or returned to the upright position.

The seat was never available on the late model convertibles. A positive locking hand operated latch was added to the seat for the 1968 and 1969 model years.

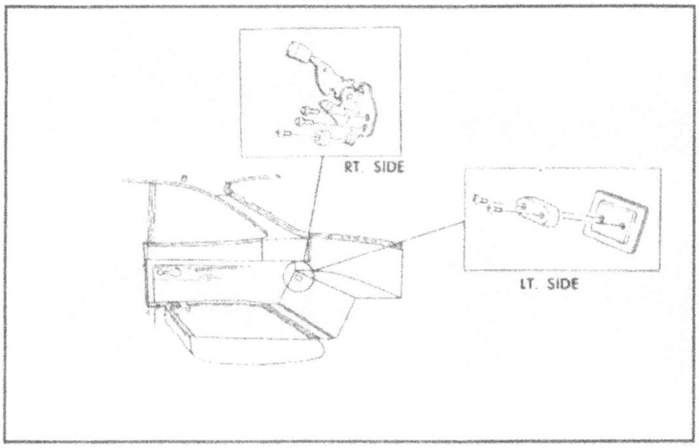

Drawing 14-10 in the Chevrolet Chassis and Parts Catalog (1976) details the rear seat positive locking device used on all models in 1968 and 1969.

Seat Belts

Lap seat belts for the front seat passengers were first offered as optional equipment in 1962. Seat belts as optional items continued through 1963.

In 1964, front seat belts became standard equipment. A "custom deluxe" seat belt was offered for the front seat. The belt included an automatic retractor and a chrome plated buckle.

Rear seat lap belts were offered as options for the first time in 1965. They came in "custom" and "custom deluxe". The custom belt buckle was color coded to the interior. Rear seat belts did not come with retractors. Seat belts with and without retractors were offered for the front seats

Dual lap belts, front and rear, were made standard equipment on all models in 1966. "Custom deluxe" belts were offered as an option. They came with retractors and bright buckles. A shoulder belt, that was completely independent of the lap belt, was offered for the first time in 1966. It was available for the front seat only and required its own buckle. The wearer had to fasten and unfasten the two belts independently.

By 1967 the retractors for the front seat belts had become standard equipment. "Custom deluxe" seat belts were offered both front and rear, and a center seat belt for the rear seat was optional. Shoulder belts were still optional items.

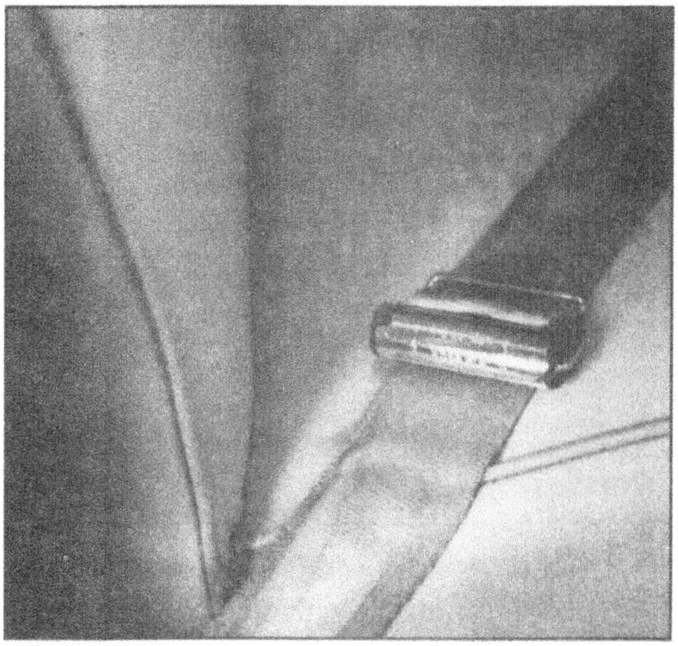

This simple seat belt retractor was photographed on a 1965 500 model.

The bright metal seat belt buckle on this 1965 Corsa featured the Fisher Body emblem.

By government decree, front seat shoulder belts with lap belts became mandatory on all cars sold after January 1, 1968. Convertibles were exempted from the rule, so shoulder belts were still offered as options on those cars. A deluxe seat belt package was still an option for all models.

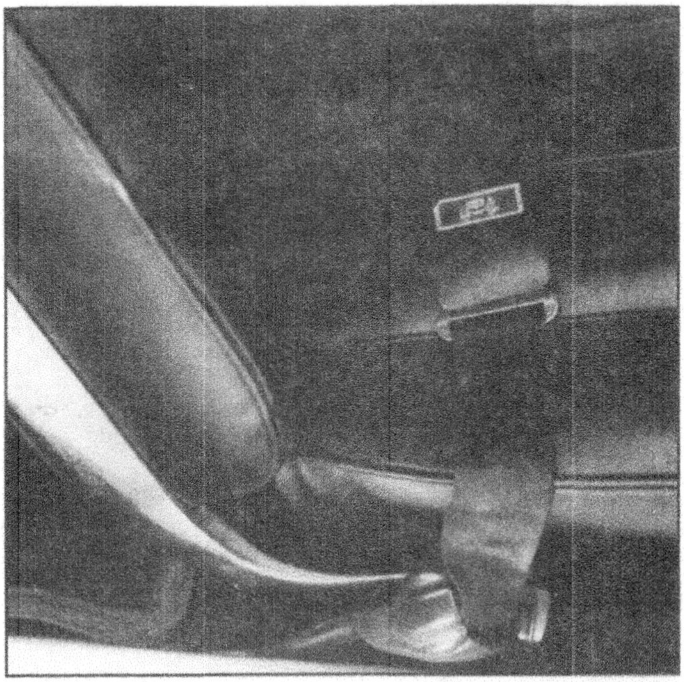

The seat belt buckle on this 1966 Corsa matched the interior color scheme.

Note the plain belt buckle emblazoned with the G.M. "Mark of Excellence" on this 1969 500. shoulder belt is in the roof.

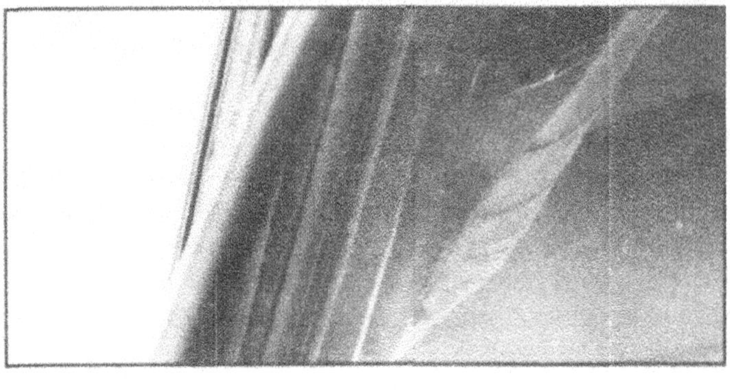

Door Related Items

Door panels were made of a composition material and covered in a vinyl fabric that carried the same pattern as the other upholstery. The door panels of the rear doors, or the rear seat sidewalls of the two door models, were finished the same as the front door panels.

The 1960 500 model door panel was a plain gray vinyl material that reflected the austere image of the car. We found the same door panel on a 1960 700 four door sedan. The armrest was optional equipment on the 500 and standard on the 700.

This multi-colored door panel on a 1960 700 two door model was eyecatching. We found identical door panels on the 1961 two and four door models.

(left)
The anchor for the 1969 shoulder beltwas in the roof.

The horizontal pleats on the door panels of the Monza complemented the stylish appearance of this model. Note the chrome plated strip on the armrest.

The 1962, Monza door panels sported a wide brushed metal band. The band immediately caught the eye of prospective buyers. It divided plain vinyl fabric below from an upper panel decorated with pleats and buttons that matched the seat covering.

The 1962 Monza door panels (front above-back below) were highlighted with a wide bright metal trim strip.

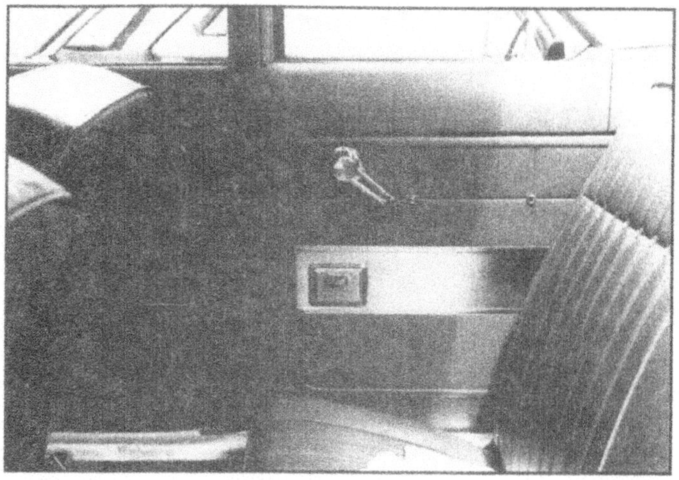

The rear seat side panel of the 1962 Monza reflected the same design as the door panels.

For 1963, the Monza seats were complimented by matching door panels that combined full length horizontal pleats with newly designed accent buttons.

A model logo appeared on the door panels for the first time in 1964. It was located above the armrest on a smooth section of vinyl.

The 1964 Monza and Spyder models had map pockets in the front door panels.

One third of the 1964 Monza upper door panel was pleated. A narrow, bright metal strip ran the full length of the door panel. The vinyl below this strip was smooth and without decoration.

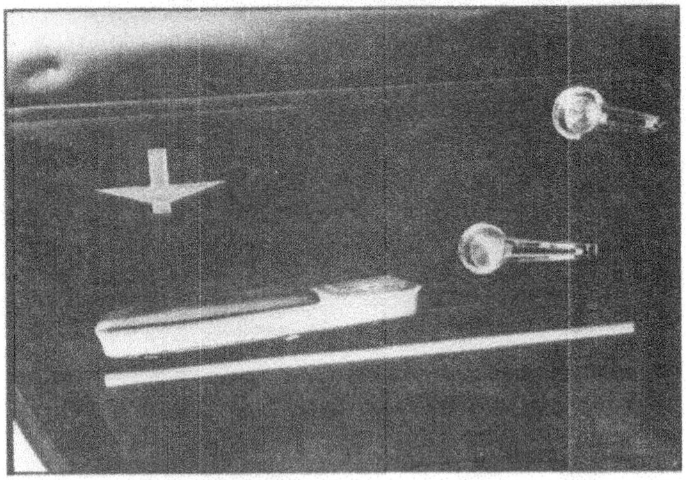

The rear door panel of this 1964 Monza mirrors the front door panel design. Note the ashtray in the armrest.

The 500 model door panel reflected the styling changes for 1965. The panel had a smooth clean look that matched the rest of the car. A wide contrasting horizontal strip divided the panel.

A metal identification plate bearing the word "Corvair" was mounted above the strip.

The door panel upholstery for the Monza and Corsa included full length horizontal pleats. The model logo was centered near the top of the panel. The map pocket became more conspicuous in the lower portion of the door. The logo was absent from the rear door of four door models.

These two photographs show the front door (above) and the rear door (below) panels of the 1965 Monza. Note the chrome plated ashtray in the rear door. armrest.

The upholstery pattern on the 1965 Corsa door was the same as the Monza. The Corsa logo distinguished the model.

The 1966 500 model door panels had a pleated design of contrasting colors. No model designations appeared on the door.

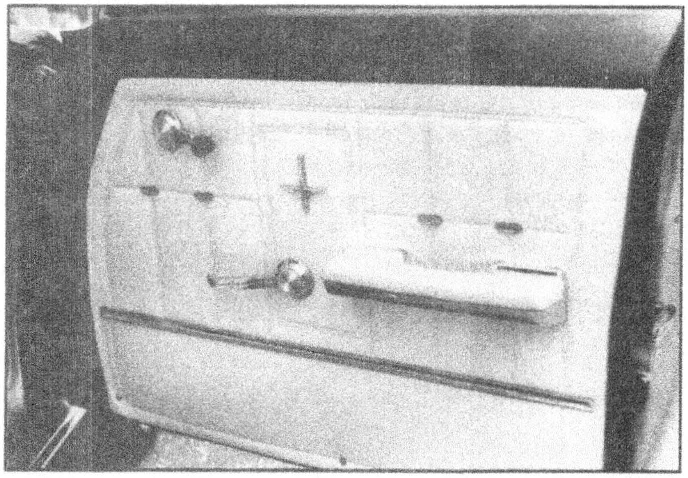

Elliptical decorative buttons, a series emblem, and checkerboard pleats graced the door panels of the 1966 Monza (above) and Corsa models.

The major change for 1967 was that the model logo was centered above the arm rest and the pleat design was changed slightly.

The design of the 1969 door panel for the 500 model was stylish. An accent strip divided the door panel while classic pleats outlined a smooth vinyl insert.

A Corvair nameplate was centered above the large armrest on the 1969 500 door panel.

In the final year of production the door panel sported box pleats above the armrest and horizontal pleats below. Rectangular decorative buttons were placed in the intersections of the box pleats. The Monza model emblem was placed forward of the door handle.

By 1969 the armrests on the 500 and Monza (above) were identical.

Armrests

In the first Corvairs, armrests were optional items on the 500 and 700 series. Chrome trimmed armrests were a standard upgrade offered only on the Monza.

Front armrests became standard equipment on all models of the Corvair in 1962. They were color coordinated with the interior. Monza armrests had the same bright trim as the previous years. No coupe models had rear armrests. They were optional equipment on the 700 sedans and station wagons and were furnished on the Monza sedans and wagons.

In 1964, front armrests were still standard equipment on all models. Rear armrests with built in ashtrays were optional items on the 700 sedan. The Monza sedan and convertible, as well as the Spyder convertible, came equipped with rear armrests featuring built-in ashtrays.

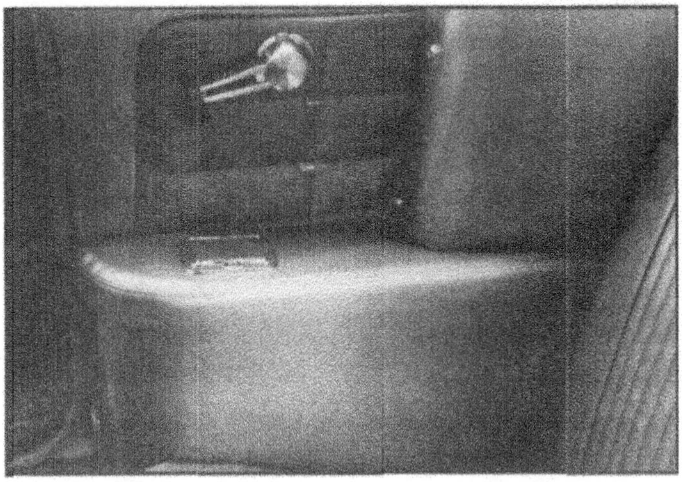

The 1963 (above) and 1964 convertibles had an ashtray and armrest built into the sidewall that hid the folding top mechanism.

Front armrests continued to be standard issue on all 1965 through 1969 Corvairs. The rear armrests with built in ashtrays were offered as optional equipment on the 500 four door sedans, but were standard equipment on the Monza and Corsa four door sedans. It appears from the literature that the rear armrests became standard equipment from 1967 until the end of production.

The two door sedan models did not have rear arm rests but had ashtrays built into the side panels. The convertibles did not have armrests per se. The side panels had indentations that served as armrests.

In 1968 the armrests were redesigned to incorporate the door handle. This was done more to comply with safety mandates than for style. They were heavily padded and carried a chrome decorative strip. The 1969 armrest was identical to the previous year except the decorative strip was removed.

Door Handles and Window Cranks

Interior door handles and window cranks changed very little in design, appearance or location during the first five years. The ventipane was opened and closed with a hand operated friction latch.

The door handles and window crank arms were chrome plated "pot metal". The knob of the window crank was black plastic on all models. The window crank was located below and forward of the door handle. The window was opened by turning the crank counter clockwise.

The door handle was located on a line with the edge of the ventipane just below the edge of the vinyl door panel. The door was opened by pulling the handle up and to the rear. On all early models the front doors were locked by pushing the handle forward.

The location of the front door handle and window crank was the same for each model from 1960 through 1964.

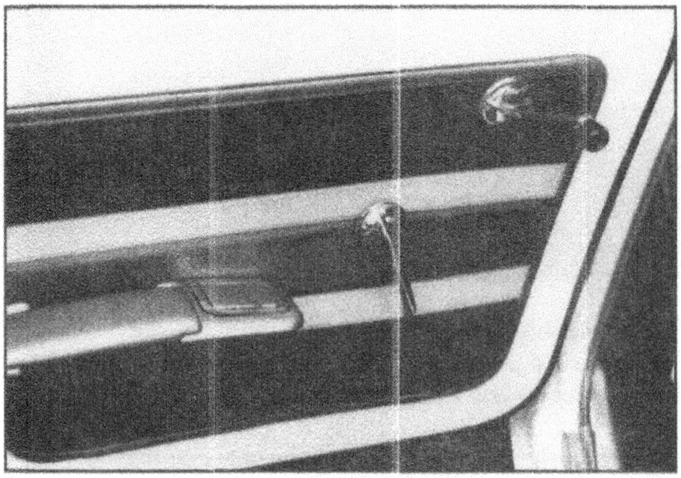

The location of the rear door handles and window cranks, as shown on this 1961 700, remained the same for all models 1960 through 1964.

On four door models, the rear window crank was located just below the top forward corner of the vinyl door panel. The door handle was located below and to the rear of the window crank, just above and forward of the arm rest.

The window cranks for the rear window of two door models were located on the side wall in the upper forward corner of the trim panel.

The design changed from a solid handle and crank arm in 1960 to a slotted design in 1962. There were no further design changes through 1964.

In 1965, the window crank arm was moved higher on the door and slightly to the rear. The door handle was moved closer to the leading edge of the arm rest.

The door handles and window cranks used in 1965 were similar to the previous year. However, the arms were solid.

This photograph of a 1965 Monza rear door shows the location of the handle and window crank.

On four door models the rear window crank arm was located in the upper front corner of the door panel. The door handle was located just in front of the arm rest. Both the front and rear doors were opened by pulling the handle up.

Interior Door Locks

The early Corvairs did not have front door lock buttons. The doors were locked from the inside by pushing the door handle forward. The rear door of the four door models had a simple push button lock. The lock button was located below the window on the forward edge of the window frame.

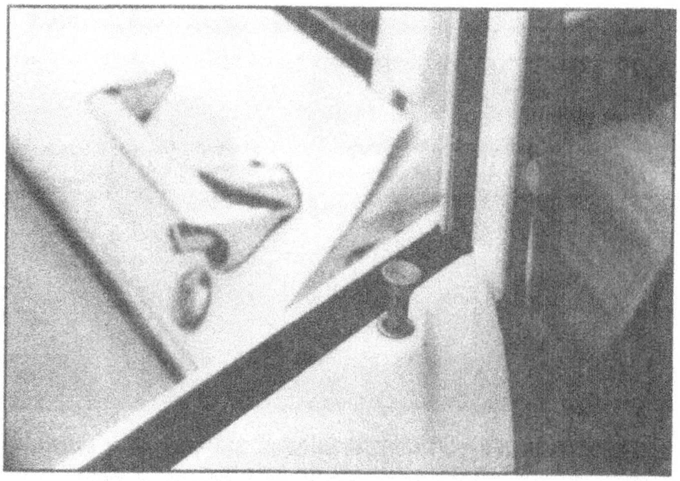

The lock buttons were color keyed to match the interior.

"Child proof" lock knobs were a dealer supplied option.

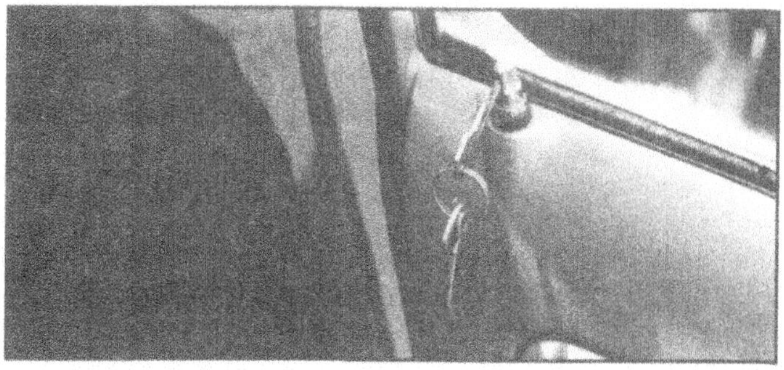

Simple push button locks were offered for all doors in 1965.

In response to vehicle safety mandates, the door lock buttons of the 1968 and 1969 models were made larger. It was reasoned that the larger buttons would cause a less serious puncture wound in an accident.

Headliner

The first 500 series Corvair came with a gray cloth headliner that matched the rest of the interior. The upscale 700 model cloth headliner was color coordinated with one of the three optional interior colors. The Monza headliner was finished in the same high quality vinyl as the rest of the interior.

The cloth headliners of the 1961 through 1964 500 and 700 series matched the available interior colors. The Monza continued with a vinyl, leather grained, headliner that matched the interior colors.

The headliner of the 1965 500 was of the same vinyl material as the seats. The vinyl headliner of the 1965 Monza and Corsa was of higher quality than the 500 model. The headliners continued to match the interior fabrics throughout the remainder of production.

Coat Hooks

Coat hooks were not offered on the 1960 500 series. They were standard equipment on all other models except the convertibles. Coat hooks were mounted above the rear side window. They rusted easily.

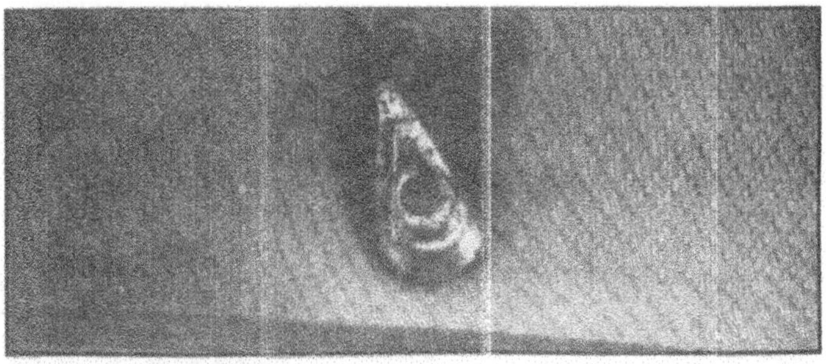

The coat hooks for the first generation Corvairs were very poor quality.

Coat hooks became standard on all models with the big change over in 1965. They appeared no different than the thin, lightly chrome plated sheet metal hooks used on early models.

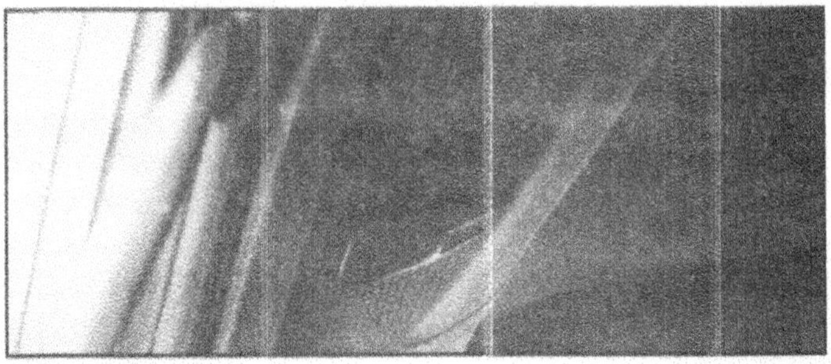

This plastic coat hook was on a 1969 500 model. It was color keyed to the interior. We suspect the coat hook was used on a variety of G.M. products of the period.

Interior Lights

An interior "dome" light was standard equipment on all Corvair models except convertibles. The light was centered in the headliner. It was activated by turning the light knob on the dash on the 500 models.

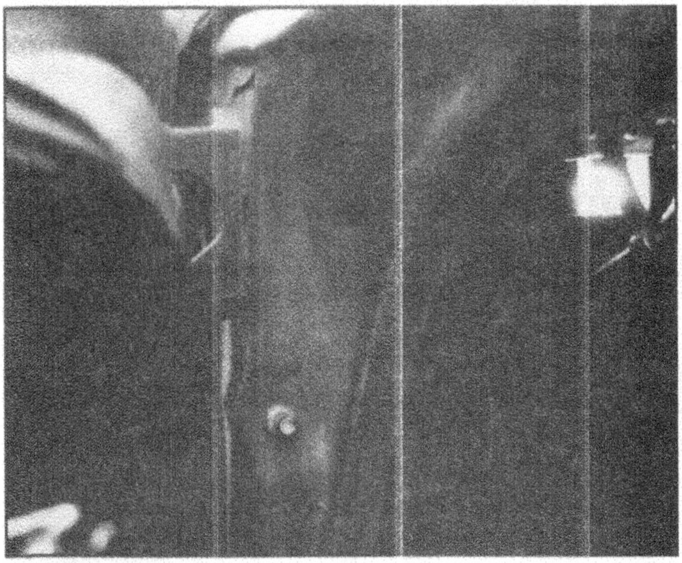

Beginning in 1961, the light was activated by a door switch on all models except the 500. Note the courtesy light under the dash.

The lens was white translucent plastic and the base on the 500 model was painted gray to match the interior. On the 700 and Monza models, the plastic base was chrome plated.

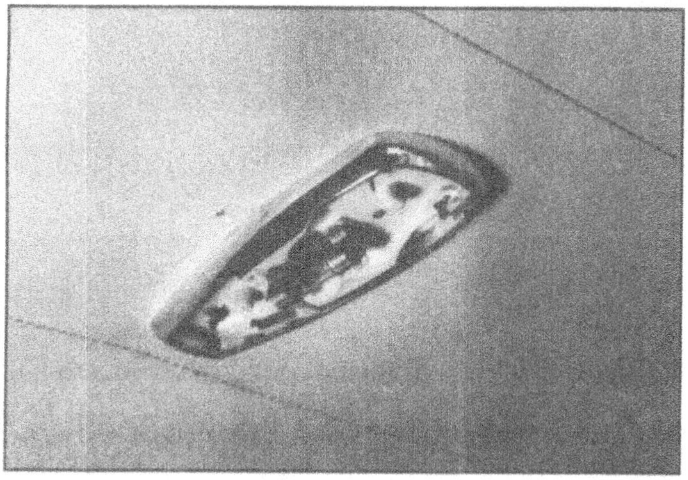

This dome light was on a 1963 Monza. The lens was removed to show the socket and mounting details.

As late as 1965, the dash switch was still necessary to turn on the dome light on the 500 models. The door switch was relocated in 1965 for the Monza and Corsa models.

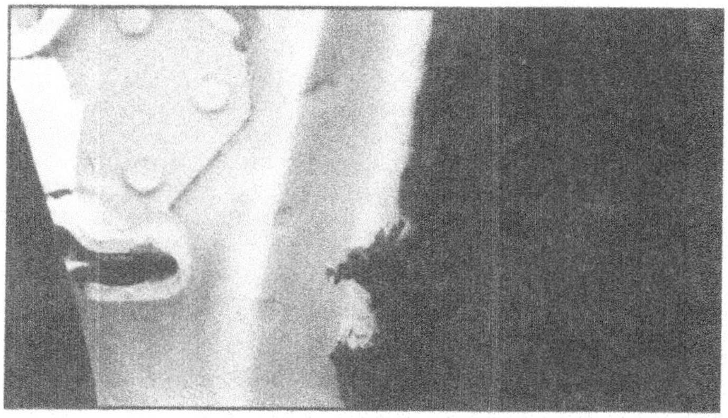

The door switch for the Monza and Corsa was mounted higher on the door frame than in earlier years.

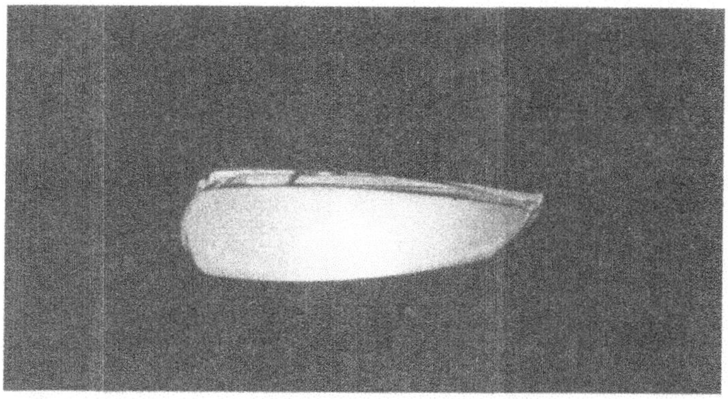

This dome light was photographed in a 1966 Monza.

Courtesy lights located under each side of the dash were factory installed options for the 700 and Monza models starting in 1961. They were operated by a door activated switch. The 1962 Monza and Spyder convertibles came with courtesy lights as standard equipment. In the late model Corvairs, courtesy lights continued to be a standard feature on convertibles, but were optional equipment on all other models.

A glove box light was optional equipment on the early 500 and 700 models, but standard on the Monza. This held true through the 1964 production year.

By 1965 the glove box light was standard issue on all models except the Corvair 500. The glove box light continued to be standard on all except the bottom of the line 500 model through 1969.

From 1967 through 1969, an interesting light group was offered. It consisted of courtesy lights under the dash, a glove compartment light, an ash tray light, a light in the luggage compartment, and a light in the engine compartment.

Pedals

The brake, clutch and gas pedals on all Corvairs were strictly utilitarian. The early manual transmission models had identical clutch and brake pedals. They were suspended from above, not sprouted out of the firewall.

The rubber pedal pads were fitted over a metal base and were easily replaced.

The pedal pads measured 3.25 inches across the top. The bottom edge of the pad measured 2.75 inches, making the pedals slightly wider at the top than the bottom. The pads were 2.50 inches long.

The single brake pedal on cars equipped with an automatic transmission measured about 2.50 inches x

5 inches. The gas pedal was long and narrow and was attached to the accelerator linkage at the base. The pedal on the cars equipped with an automatic transmission were the same size as those with a manual transmission.

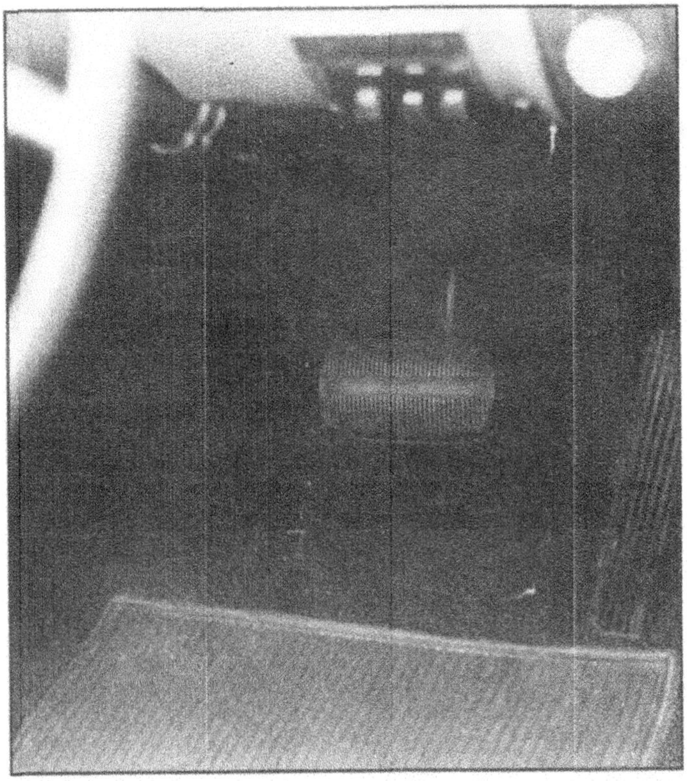

The post-1964 models showed very little change in pedal design or size. These pedals also had the replaceable rubber caps.

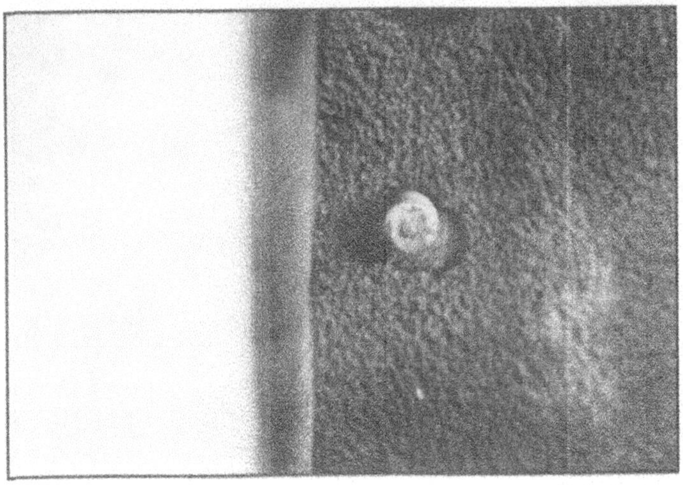

The bright lights were operated by a floor mounted dimmer switch. This switch remained the same from 1960 through 1969.

Shift Levers

The floor mounted manual shift lever with the goose neck curve was a unique feature for the Corvair at a time when most other American car shifters were mounted on the steering column. It gave even the economy 500 of 1960 a little extra pizzazz. The stick shift of all manual transmission models had a small black knob with the shifting diagram engraved on it.

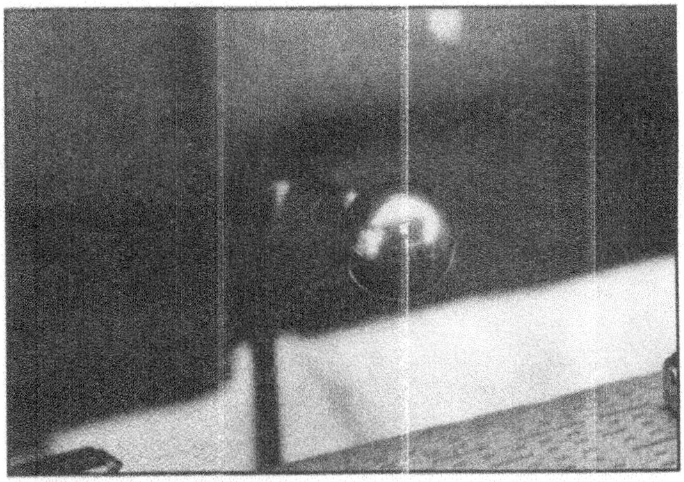

The manual transmission had three forward gears and a reverse gear.

Powerglide two-speed automatic transmission was offered as an option. The automatic transmission offered two forward ranges, a reverse, and a neutral selection.

The control lever of the automatic transmission was mounted on the right side of the instrument panel.

The 1961 models used the same design for both the stick shift and the automatic transmission as was used in the previous year. The standard three speed manual and automatic transmissions were now augmented by an optional four speed manual transmission.

The three speed transmission stick had a black knob and the four speed was crowned with a white knob.

In 1962, the three speed and four speed manual transmissions and the automatic were once again offered. The four speed manual transmission was standard on the Spyder models.

The shifter knob color scheme remained the same in 1963 and the same transmission selections were also available. Minor refinements were all that were made in 1964 as a three speed transmission was once again standard and the automatic and four speed manual transmissions were optional.

The three-speed, four-speed, and automatic transmission options were still available in 1965. The Powerglide automatic transmission was not offered with the 180 horsepower turbocharged engine. Even with a radical restyling of the instrument panel, the Powerglide shift lever kept it's place on the right side of the instruments and left of the centered radio.

The 1965 through 1969 automatic transmission option offered two forward ranges, a neutral and a reverse selection.

The black/white shift knobs were used on the three and four speed floor shifters as in the past. Corsas were distinguished by a chrome plated shifter cover plate. The Monza sported a rubber boot and the lowly 500 model had no decoration at the base of the stick.

No changes in the transmission availability were made for 1966. In 1967, the dash mounted range selector switch was equipped with mechanical stops. These stops eliminated unintentional shifting of the automatic transmission to low and reverse. Transmission availability and equipment remained the same until the last model was sent to a dealer in 1969.

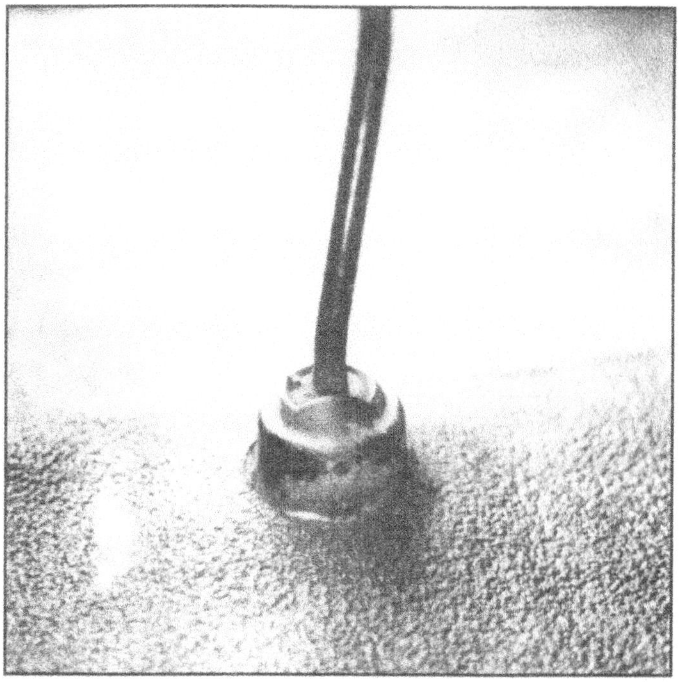

This 1969 500 manual shift lever (above) had no decorative boot. The top of the line Corsa had a chrome plated cover at the base of the shift stick (below).

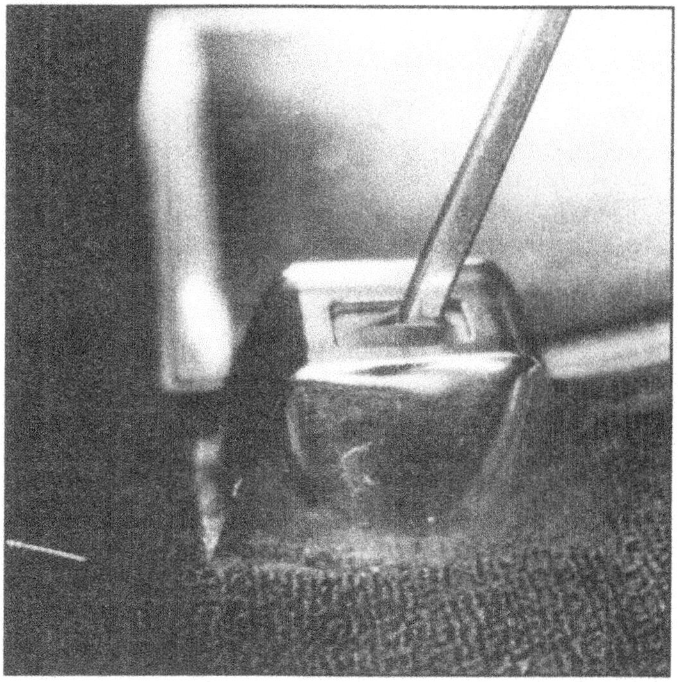

Emergency Brake

The emergency brake was located under the left side of the dash, available to the driver's left hand. It was a a hinged lever design with a squeeze trigger that released a lock. For all of the engineering advances apparent in the Corvair, the emergency brake handle was old fashioned.

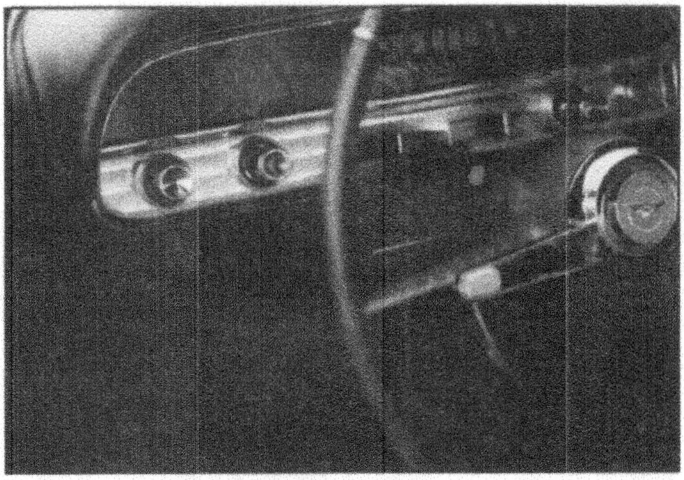

This photograph of a 1963 Monza shows the emergency brake handle in the lower left corner. The optional emergency brake warning light was located below the windshield wiper and light switches.

This photograph of a 1965 Monza illustrates that the location and design of the emergency brake carried through to the second generation.

Turn Signal Levers

Automatic turn signals were standard on all models for all years. The turn signal lever was mounted on the left side of the steering column. The lever was moved up to signal a right turn and down to signal a left turn. The designers did not waste their creative juices on the turn signal levers.

In 1967 the turn lever was redesigned so that slight pressure on the lever would allow the driver to indicate lane changes. When the pressure was released the switch would return to the neutral position.

The 1960 turn signal design was utilitarian. The plastic grip matched the lights and wiper knobs.

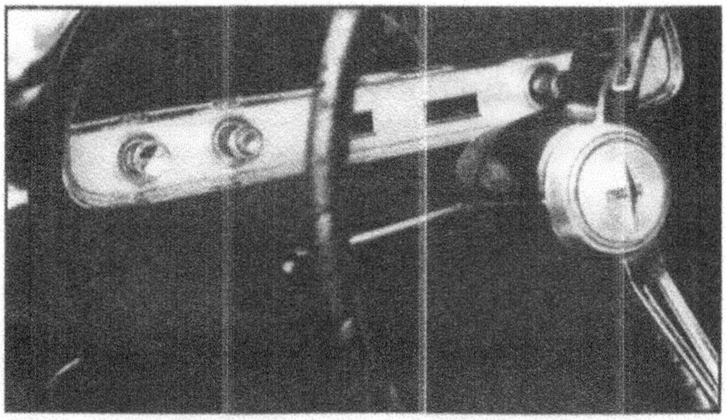

In 1964 the turn signal grips still followed the design of the dash knobs.

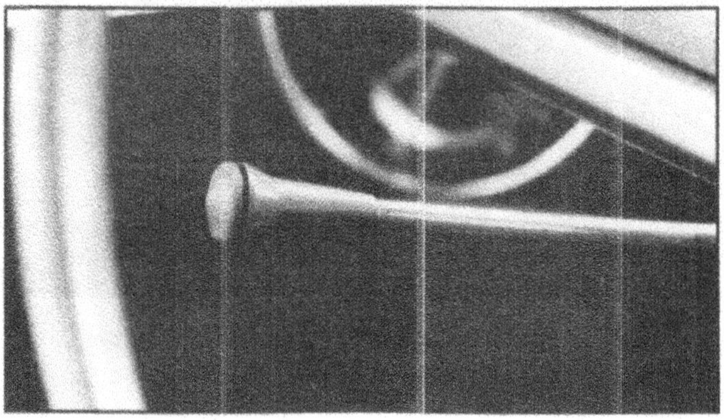

This 1969 turn signal shows that the knob was enlarged to comply with safety mandates.

Floor Mats and Carpeting

The black rubber floor mats offered the only hint of contrast to the plain gray interior of the 1960 500 Corvair. An extra bonus for purchasing the 700 series was color coordinated floor mats. Color coordinated loop pile carpet set off the Monza as the top of the line model in 1960.

In 1961, the black rubber floor mats were still standard issue, even though new interior colors were offered on the 500. Vinyl coated, color keyed floor mats were offered on the 700 models, while plush carpeted floorboards were the mark of the Monza.

No changes in mat offerings were made in 1962 since rubber floor mats continued to be standard on the 500 model. These were one of the few reminders left of the spartan years. Good quality vinyl mats were again offered on the 700 models and the Monza continued with plush carpeting. The floor coverings offered in 1963 and 1964 were very similar to those found in 1962.

Color keyed rubber floor mats were standard equipment on the 1965 and 1966 500 series. A high quality loop pile carpet of a harmonizing color completed the pleasing interior of the Monza and Corsa models for both 1965 and 1966. The same, or very similar, floor coverings were offered during the last three years of production.

Chapter 6

Paint and Trim

EXTERIOR PAINT AND INTERIOR TRIM COMBINATIONS

The Corvair designers certainly did not lack for creativity or versatility when it came to designating or naming exterior paint options. Unfortunately, in this writer's opinion, the exterior paint coding did not always follow the same common sense system as the other numbering schemes.

From 1960 through 1964, the color code numbers seem to make some sense. Paint colors are an easy way to differentiate model years, but some colors are so similar despite name and number changes, that the common car buyer would have difficulty distinguishing the changes from one year to the next.

From 1965 through 1968, the letter designations are very confusing. The same letter means different colors for different years. To make sure the same paint color is used, it is necessary to know the vehicle year, the color name and letter designation. This information can then be matched to the color number for one of the three or four companies that supplied paint to Chevrolet. The 1969 color system returned to an understandable numbering code.

We were not able to find the various interior trim combinations that were offered for specific exterior colors for all years. Some sources have suggested that for those years, Chevrolet may have offered any interior color with any exterior color. We doubt that was the case and suggest that our research just failed to turn up the color combinations offered. We apologize for the incomplete information.

1960 COLOR AND TRIM COMBINATIONS			
EXTERIOR COLOR AND CODE	**INTERIOR COLOR**		
	500	**700**	**MONZA**
Cascade Green (903)	Gray	Blue	Blue
Crocus Cream (925)		Gray	Green
Ermine White (936)		Green	Red
Horizon Blue (910)			Turquoise
Jade Green (905)			
Roman Red (923)			
Royal Blue (912)			
Sateen Silver (940)			
Tasco Turquoise (915)			
Tuxedo Black (900)			

1961 COLOR AND TRIM COMBINATIONS			
EXTERIOR COLOR AND CODE	INTERIOR COLOR AND TRIM NAMES & CODE		
	500	700	MONZA
Almond Beige (938)	Blue (836) or (837)	Blue (888) or (898)	REGULAR SEATS
Arbor Green (905)	Gray (885) or (895)	Gray (886) or (896)	Blue (829) or (858)
Coronna Cream (925)	Green (831) or (832)	Green (887) or (897)	Fawn (816) or (855)
Fawn Beige (920)		Red (889) or (899)	Gray (830) or (844)
Ermine White (936)			Green (821) or (847) or (857)
Honduras Maroon (948)			Ivory (859)
Jewel Blue (912)			Red (820) or (856)
Midnight Blue (914)			
Roman Red (923)			BUCKET SEATS
Sateen Silver (940)			Fawn (845) or (880)
Seafoam Green (903)			Red (846) or (881)
Seamist Turquoise (917)			Green (847) or (882)
Shadow Gray (941)			Blue (848) or (883)
Tuxedo Black (900)			Gray (870) or (871)
Twilight Turquoise (915)			Black (878)
			Ivory (879)

1961 TRIM CODES

500 2 DR & 4 DR – 527-569 REGULAR SEATS

Blue (836) Medium blue cloth with medium metallic blue or light blue vinyl leather

Gray (885) Medium gray cloth with light gray or ivory vinyl leather

Green (831) Medium green cloth with medium metallic green or light green vinyl leather

500 STATION WAGON – 535 REGULAR SEATS

Blue (837) Medium metallic blue fibre rib vinyl leather or medium metallic blue & light blue vinyl leather

Gray (895) Light metallic gray fiber rib vinyl leather or light gray & ivory vinyl leather

Green (832) Medium metallic green fibre rib vinyl leather or medium metallic green and light green vinyl leather

1961 TRIM CODES

700 2 DR AND 4 DR – 727-69 REGULAR SEATS

Blue (888) Medium blue cloth with medium metallicblue vinyl leather

Gray (886) Medium gray cloth with light gray and ivory vinyl leather

Green (887) Medium green cloth with medium metallic green vinyl leather

Red (889) Red cloth with red vinyl leather

700 STATION WAGON – 735 REGULAR SEATS

Blue (898) Medium blue cloth with medium metallic blue vinyl leather

Gray (896) Medium gray cloth with light gray and ivory vinyl leather

Green (897) Medium green cloth with medium metallic green vinyl leather

Red (899) Red cloth with red vinyl leather

MONZA 2 DR – 927 BUCKET SEATS

Black (878) Black vinyl leather

Blue (883) Medium blue metallic vinyl leather

Fawn (880) Medium fawn metallic vinyl leather

Green (882) Medium green metallic vinyl leather

Ivory (879) Ivory vinyl leather

Red (881) Red vinyl leather

MONZA 4 DR – 969 BUCKET SEATS

Blue (848) Medium blue cloth with medium blue metallic vinyl leather

Fawn (845) Medium fawn cloth with medium fawn metallic vinyl leather

Gray (870) Light gray cloth with black vinyl leather

Gray (871) Light gray cloth with ivory vinyl leather

Green (847) Medium green cloth with medium green vinyl leather

Red (846) Red cloth with red vinyl leather

MONZA 4 DR – 969 REGULAR SEATS

Blue (829) Medium blue cloth with medium metallic blue vinyl leather

Blue (858) Medium metallic blue vinyl leather

Fawn (816) Medium fawn cloth with medium metallic fawn vinyl leather

Fawn (855) Medium metallic fawn vinyl leather

Gray (830) Light gray cloth with black vinyl leather

Gray (844) Light gray cloth with ivory vinyl leather

Green (821) Medium green cloth with medium metallic green vinyl leather

Green (847) Medium green cloth with medium metallic green vinyl leather

Green (857) Medium metallic green vinyl leather

Ivory (859) Ivory vinyl leather

Red (820) Red cloth with red vinyl leather

Red (856) Red vinyl leather

1962 COLOR AND TRIM COMBINATIONS			
EXTERIOR COLOR AND CODE	**INTERIOR COLOR AND TRIM NAME & CODE**		
	500	**700**	**MONZA AND SPYDER**
Adobe Beige (938) Anniversary Gold (927) Autumn Gold (920) Coronna Cream (925) Ermine White (936) Laurel Green (905) Nassau Blue (914) Roman Red (923) Satin Silver (940) Silver Blue (912) Surf Green (903) Tuxedo Black (900) Twilight Turquoise (918)	Aqua (745) Fawn (756) Red (779)	Aqua (751) Blue (731) Fawn (757) Red (780)	REGULAR SEATS Aqua (748) Blue (735) Fawn (759) Gold (793) Red (782) BUCKET SEATS Aqua (719) & (755) Black (712) & (715) Blue (732) & (736) Fawn (758) & (769) Gold (795) & (799) Red (781) & (785)

<u>500 2 DR – 527 BENCH SEATS</u>

Aqua (745) Aqua cloth with aqua metallic vinyl leather

Fawn (756) Fawn cloth with fawn metallic vinyl leather

Red (779) Red cloth with red vinyl leather

<u>700 ALL BODY STYLES – 727, 735, 769 BENCH SEATS</u>

Aqua (751) Aqua cloth with aqua metallic vinyl leather or light aqua vinyl leather

Blue (731) Medium blue cloth with dark metallic blue vinyl leather or light blue vinyl leather

Fawn (757) Medium fawn cloth with dark metallic fawn vinyl leather or light fawn vinyl leather

Red (780) Medium red cloth with dark red and ivory vinyl leather

<u>MONZA 4 DR SEDAN AND WAGON – 969 & 935 BENCH SEATS</u>

Aqua (748) Aqua cloth with aqua metallic vinyl leather

Blue (735) Medium blue cloth with medium blue metallic vinyl leather

Fawn (759) Medium fawn cloth with medium fawn metallic vinyl leather

Gold (793) Light gold cloth with light gold vinyl leather

Red (782) Red cloth with red vinyl leather

<u>MONZA 2 DR AND CONVERTIBLE – 927 & 967 BUCKET SEATS</u>

Aqua (755) Aqua metallic vinyl leather

Black (712) Black vinyl leather

Blue (732) Medium blue metallic vinyl leather

Fawn (758) Medium fawn vinyl leather

Gold (795) Light gold vinyl leather

1962 TRIM CODES

MONZA 4 DR AND STATION WAGON – 969 & 935 BUCKET SEATS

Aqua (719) Aqua metallic vinyl leather

Black (715) Black vinyl leather

Blue (736) Medium blue metallic vinyl leather

Fawn (769) Medium fawn metallic vinyl leather

Red (785) Red metallic vinyl leather

Gold (799) Light gold vinyl leather (4 door model only)

1963 COLOR AND TRIM COMBINATIONS			
EXTERIOR COLOR AND CODE	INTERIOR COLOR AND TRIM NAME & CODE		
	500	700	MONZA &SPYDER
Adobe Beige (938) Azure Aqua (918) Autumn Gold (920) Cordovan Brown (934) Ember Red (922) Ermine White (936) Ivy Green (908) Laurel Green (905) Marina Aqua (919) Monaco Blue (914) Palomar Red (948) Saddle Tan (932) Silver Blue (912) Tuxedo Black (900)	Aqua (720) Fawn (764) Red (783)	Aqua (751) Blue (731) Fawn (757) Red (780)	<u>BUCKET SEATS</u> Aqua (755) Black (712) Blue (732) Fawn (758) Ivory (727) Red (781) Saddle (705)

1963 TRIM CODES

<u>500 2 DR – 527 BENCH SEATS</u>

Aqua (720) Medium metallic aqua vinyl leather or light aqua vinyl leather

Fawn (764) Medium metallic fawn vinyl leather or light fawn vinyl leather

Red (783) Red vinyl leather or ivory vinyl leather

<u>700 2 DR AND 4 DOOR – 727 & 769 BENCH SEATS</u>

Aqua (751) Medium aqua cloth with light aqua vinyl leather

Blue (731) Medium blue cloth with light blue vinyl leather

Fawn (757) Medium fawn cloth with light fawn vinyl leather

Red (780) Red cloth with ivory vinyl leather

<u>MONZA 2 DR, 4 DR, AND CONVERTIBLE – 927, 967 & 969 BUCKET SEATS</u>

Aqua (755) Medium aqua vinyl leather

Black (712) Black vinyl leather

Blue (732) Medium metallic blue vinyl leather

Fawn (758) Medium metallic fawn vinyl leather

Ivory (727) Ivory vinyl leather

Red (781) Red vinyl leather

Saddle (705) Medium saddle vinyl leather

1964 COLOR AND TRIM COMBINATIONS			
EXTERIOR COLOR AND CODE	**INTERIOR COLOR AND TRIM NAME & CODE**		
	500 MODEL	**700 MODEL**	**MONZA & SPYDER**
Almond Fawn (920)*	Fawn (764)	Fawn (757)	Black (712) Fawn (758) Saddle (705)
Azure Aqua (918)*	Aqua (720)	Aqua#	Aqua (755) Black (712)
Bahama Green (908)*	Fawn (764)	Fawn (757)	Fawn (758) Saddle (705)
Daytona Blue (916)*	Fawn (764)	Blue (731)	Black (712) Blue (732)
Desert Beige (938)	Fawn (764) Red (783)	Fawn (757) Red (751) Red (780)	Black (712) Fawn (758) Red (781) Saddle (705)
Ember Red (922)	Fawn (764) Red (783)	Fawn (757) Red (751) Red (780)	Black (712) Fawn (758) Red (781) Ivory (727)
Ermine White (936)	Aqua (720) Fawn (764) Red (783)	Blue (731) Fawn (757) Red (751) Red (780)	Aqua (755) Black (712) Blue (732) Fawn (758) Red (781) Saddle (705) Ivory (727)
Goldwin Yellow (943)	Not Offered	Not Offered	Black (712)
Lagoon Aqua (919)	Aqua (720)	Aqua #	Aqua (755)
Meadow Green (905)*	Fawn (764)	Fawn (757)	Black (712) Fawn (758)
Palomar Red (948)*	Fawn (764) Red (783)	Fawn (757) Red (751) Red (780)	Black (712) Fawn (758) Red (781) Ivory (727)
Saddle Tan (932)*	Fawn (764)	Fawn (757)	Fawn (758) Saddle (705)
Satin Silver (940)*	Aqua (720) Red (783)	Blue (731) Red (783) Red (780)	Aqua (755) Black (712) Blue (732) Red (781) Ivory (727)
Silver Blue (912)*	Fawn (764)	Blue (731)	Black (712) Blue (732)
Tuxedo Black (900)	Aqua (720) Fawn (764) Red (783)	Blue (731) Fawn (757) Red (783) Red (780)	Aqua (755) Black (712) Blue (732) Fawn (758) Red (781) Ivory (727) Saddle (705)

1964 TWO-TONE COLOR AND TRIM COMBINATIONS 500 & 700 MODELS ONLY		
EXTERIOR COLOR & CODE	**INTERIOR COLOR & TRIM CODES**	
	500	**700**
Azure Aqua* over Ermine White (988)	Aqua (720)	Aqua #
Bahama Green* over Meadow Green (952)	Fawn (764)	Fawn (757)
Daytona Blue* over Satin Silver (982)	Fawn (764)	Blue (731)
Daytona Blue* over Silver Blue (960)	Fawn (764)	Blue (731)
Desert Beige over Ember Red (975)	Fawn (764) Red (783)	Fawn (757) Red (780)
Desert Beige over Palomar Red* (993)	Fawn (764)	Fawn (757)
Desert Beige over Saddle Tan* (971)	Fawn (764)	Fawn (757)
ErmineWhite over Lagoon Aqua* (965)	Aqua (720)	Aqua #
Ermine White over Meadow Green* (954)	Fawn (764)	Fawn (757)
Ermine White over Silver Blue* (959)	Fawn (764)	Blue (731)
Satin Silver* over Palomar Red* (995)	Red (783)	Red (780)

Not described in the Chevrolet Parts Catalogue. Other sources noted an aqua interior option for the 700 model.
* Metallic paint
All Monza and Spyders equipped with all vinyl interior with front bucket seats standard. Ivory interior offered on Monza and Monza Spyder models only. The ivory interior included a red instrument panel, red steering wheel, and red carpeting
White was the standard color for all convertible tops, black or beige was a no cost option for all exterior colors. The boot was always the same color as the interior.

500 2 DR – 527 BENCH SEATS

Aqua (720) Metallic medium aqua vinyl leather

Fawn (764) Light fawn vinyl leather

Red (783) Medium red W/ pattern vinyl leather

700 4 DR – 769 BENCH SEATS

Blue (731) Medium blue scotia cloth with metallic medium blue vinyl leather

Fawn (757) Medium fawn scotia cloth with light fawn vinyl leather

Red (751) Medium red scotia cloth and vinyl leather

SPYDER 2 DR AND CONVERTIBLE – 627 & 667; MONZA 2 DR, 4 DR AND CONVERTIBLE – 927 & 967 & 969 BUCKET SEATS

Aqua (755) Metallic medium aqua vinyl leather

Black (712) Black vinyl leather

Blue (732) Medium metallic blue vinyl leather

Fawn (758) Light fawn vinyl leather

Ivory (727) Ivory vinyl leather

Red (781) Medium red vinyl leather

Saddle (705) Medium saddle vinyl leather

1965 COLOR AND TRIM COMBINATIONS		
EXTERIOR COLOR AND CODE	**INTERIOR COLOR AND TRIM CODES**	
	500	**MONZA & CORSA**
Artesian Turquoise (K) Cameo Beige (V) Crocus Yellow (Y) Cypress Green (J) Danube Blue (E) Ermine White (C) Evening Orchid (P) Glacier Gray (W) Madeira Maroon (N) Mist Blue (D) Regal Red (R) Sierra Tan (S) Tahitian Turquoise (L) Tuxedo Black (A) Willow Green (H)	Fawn (771) Red (782) Turquoise (723)	BUCKET SEATS ONLY Black (713) Blue (733) Fawn (773) Ivory (797) & (798) Red (785) Saddle (706) Slate (795)

1965 TRIM CODES

500 2 DR AND 4 DR – Bench Seats

Fawn (771) Light fawn pattern vinyl leather

Red (782) Red pattern vinyl leather

Turquoise (723) Turquoise pattern vinyl leather

MONZA and CORSA 2 DR, 4 DR and Convertible – Bucket Seats

Black (713) Black vinyl leather

Blue (733) Medium blue vinyl leather

Fawn (773) Light fawn vinyl leather

Ivory (797) Ivory vinyl leather (Corsa only)

Ivory (798) Ivory vinyl leather (Monza only)

Red (785) Red vinyl leather

Slate (795) Slate vinyl leather

1966 COLOR AND TRIM COMBINATIONS		
EXTERIOR COLOR AND CODE	INTERIOR COLOR AND TRIM CODES	
	500	MONZA AND CORSA
Artesian Turquoise (KK)	Fawn (701)	Fawn (702) Turquoise (#) Black (758) White/Black (*)
Aztec Bronze (MM)	Fawn (701)	Black (758) Bronze (788) Fawn (702)
Cameo Beige (VV)	Fawn (701)	Black (758) Bronze (788) Fawn (702)
Chateau Slate (WW)	N.A.	Black (758)White/Black (*)
Danube Blue (EE)	Blue (721)	Black (758) Fawn (702)
Ermine White (CC)	Blue (721) Fawn (701) Red (739)	Black (758) Brt. Blue (722) Bronze (788) Fawn (702) Red (740) Turquoise (#) White/Black (*)
Lemonwood Yellow (YY)	N.A.	Black (758) White/Black (*)
Maderia Maroon (NN)	Fawn (701) Red (739)	Black (758) Fawn (702) Red (740) White/Black (*)
Marina Blue (FF)	N.A.	Black (758) Bright Blue (722) White/Black (*)
Mist Blue (DD)	Blue (721)	Black (758) White/Black (*)
Regal Red (RR)	Red (739)	Black (758) Red (740) White/Black (*)
Sandalwood Tan (TT)	Fawn (701)	Black (758) Fawn (702)
Tropic Turquoise (LL)	Fawn (701)	Fawn (702) Turquoise (#)
Tuxedo Black (AA)	Blue (721) Fawn (701) Red (739)	Black (758) Brt. Blue (722) Bronze (788) Fawn (702) Red (740) Turquoise (#) White/Black (*)
Willow Green (HH)	Fawn (701)	Black (758) Fawn (702) White/Black (*)

1966 TWO TONE COLOR AND TRIM COMBINATIONS (SPORT SEDANS ONLY)		
EXTERIOR COLOR AND CODE	INTERIOR COLOR AND TRIM CODES	
	500	MONZA AND CORSA
Chateau Slate/Tuxedo Black (WA)	N.A.	Black (758)
Ermine White/Artesian Turquoise (CK)	N.A.	Turquoise (#)
Maderia Maroon/Tuxedo Black (NA)	N.A.	Black (758)
Mist Blue/Danube Blue (DE)	Blue (721)	N.A.
Mist Blue/Ermine White (DC)	Blue (721)	N.A.
Sandalwood Tan/Cameo Beige (TV)	Fawn (701)	Fawn (702)
Tropic Turquoise/Ermine White (LC)	N.A.	Turquoise (#)

1966 TRIM CODES

500 2 DR AND 4 DR – Bench seats

Fawn (701) Light fawn pattern vinyl leather

Blue (721) Medium blue pattern vinyl leather

Red (739) Red pattern vinyl leather

MONZA AND CORSA 2 DR, 4 DR and Convertible – Bucket Seats

Black (758) Black vinyl leather

Blue (722) Medium bright blue vinyl leather (Monza)
Blue (792) Medium bright blue vinyl leather (Corsa)

Bronze (788) Bronze vinyl leather

Fawn (702) Light fawn vinyl leather

Ivory (795) Ivory vinyl leather

Red (740) Red vinyl leather

Not listed in the Chevrolet Parts Catalogue. Listed as Code T in the 1966 Dealer Option catalogue.

* Not listed in the Chevrolet Parts Catalogue. Listed as Code S in the 1966 Dealer Option catalogue. The black was used for the instrument panel and carpet. Not available for Sport Sedan model.

RECOMMENDED 1967 COLOR AND TRIM COMBINATIONS		
EXTERIOR COLOR & CODE	**INTERIOR COLOR AND TRIM CODES**	
	500	**MONZA**
Bolero Red (R/R)	Black (751)	Black (758)
Butternut Yellow (Y/Y)	Black (751) Fawn (703)	Black (758)
Capri Cream (T/T)	Black (758) Fawn (703)	Black (751) Gold (713)
Deepwater Blue (E/E)	Black (751) Blue (721)	Black (758)
Emerald Turquoise (K/K)	Black (751) Fawn (703)	Black (758)
Ermine White (C/C)	Black (751) Fawn (703) Blue (721)	Black (758) Gold (713) Bright Blue (722) or (716)
Granada Gold (G/G)	Black (751) Fawn (703)	Black (758) Gold (713)
Madera Maroon (N/N)	Black (751) Fawn (703)	Black (758) Gold (713)
Marina Blue (F/F)	Black (751) Blue (721)	Black (758) Bright Blue (722) or (716)
Mountain Green (H/H)	Black (751) Fawn (703)	Black (758)
Nantucket Blue (D/D)	Black (751) Blue (721)	Black (758)
Royal Plum (M/M)	Black (751)	Black (758)
Sierra Fawn (S/S)	Black (751) Fawn (703)	Black (758) Gold (713)
Tahoe Turquoise (L/L)	Black (751) Fawn (703)	Black (758)
Tuxedo Black (A/A)	Black (758) Fawn (703) Blue (721)	Black (758) Gold (713)

Convertible tops were available in choice of black, blue, or white. Boot color matched interior color.

Note: Interior colors were recommended only. Any solid exterior color could have been ordered with any interior color, if desired.

1967 TWO TONE EXT. COMBINATIONS (SPORT SEDANS ONLY)		
	500	MONZA
Deepwater Blue / Nantucket Blue (E/D)	Blue (721)	Bright Blue (722)
Ermine White / Nantucket Blue (C/D)	Blue (721)	N.A.
Granada Gold / Capri Cream (G/T)	Black (751) or Fawn (703)	N.A.
Nantucket Blue / Deepwater Blue (D/E)	Blue (721)	N.A.
Nantucket Blue / Ermine White (D/C)	Blue (721)	Black (758) or Gold (713)
Sierra Fawn / Capri Cream (S/T)	Black (751) or Fawn (703)	Black (758) or Gold (713)
Convertible tops were available in choice of black, blue, or white. Boot color matched interior color. **Note: Interior colors were recommended only. Any solid exterior color could have been ordered with any interior color, if desired.**		

1967 TRIM CODES

500 2 DR AND 4 DR – 10137 & 10139 BENCH SEATS

Black (751) Black pattern vinyl leather

Blue (721) Medium blue pattern vinyl leather

Fawn (703) Medium fawn vinyl leather

MONZA 2 DR 4 DR AND CONVERTIBLE – 10537,10539 &10567 BUCKET SEATS

Black (758) Black vinyl leather

Bright Blue (716) Medium Bright blue vinyl leather

Gold (713) Medium gold vinyl leather

1968 COLOR AND TRIM COMBINATIONS		
EXTERIOR COLOR AND CODE	INTERIOR COLOR AND TRIM CODE	
	500	MONZA & CORSA
Ash Gold (GG)	Black (703) Gold (709)	Black (704) Gold (710)
Butternut Yellow (YY)	Black (703) Gold (709)	Black (704) Gold (710)
Cordovan Maroon (NN)	Black (703)	Black (704)
Ermine White (CC)	Black (703) Blue (706) Gold (709)	Black (704) Blue (707) Gold (710)
Grecian Green (HH)	Black (703) Gold (709)	Black (704) Gold (710)
Grotto Blue (DD)	Black (703) Blue (706)	Black (704) Blue (707)
Island Teal (FF)	Black (703) Blue (706)	Black (704) Blue (707)
Matador Red (RR)	Black (703)	Black (704)
Palomino Ivory (TT)	Black (703) Blue (706) Gold (709)	Black (704) Blue (707) Gold (710)
Phantom Blue (EE)	Black (703) Blue (706)	Black (704) Blue (707)
Seafrost Green (PP)	Black (703) Gold (709)	Black (704) Gold (710)
Sequoia Green (VV)	Black (703) Gold (709)	Black (704) Gold (710)
Teal Blue (LL)	Black (703) Blue (706)	Black (704) Blue (707)
Tripoli Turquoise (KK)	Black (703)	Black (704)
Tuxedo Black (AA)	Black (703) Blue (706) Gold (709)	Black (704) Blue (707) Gold (710)

1968 TRIM CODES

500 2 DR – 10137 BENCH SEATS

Black (703) Black patterned vinyl leather
Blue (706) Dark blue patterened vinyl leather
Gold (709) Medium gold patterened vinyl leather

500 4 DR – 10139 BENCH SEATS

The color code numbers were the same as for the two door, but the vinyl leather had a smooth surface with no pattern.

MONZA 2 DR 4 DR AND CONVERTIBLE – 10537, 10539, 10567 BUCKET SEATS

Black (704) Black vinyl leather, no pattern on upholstery
Blue (707) Dark blue vinyl leather, no pattern on upholstery
Gold (710) Medium gold vinyl leather, no pattern on upholstery

1969 COLOR AND TRIM COMBINATIONS		
EXTERIOR COLOR & NUMBER	INTERIOR COLOR & TRIM CODES	
	500	MONZA
Azure Turquoise (55)	Black (700)	Black (701)
Burgandy (67)	Black (700)	Black (701)
Burnished Brown (61)	Black (700)	Black (701)
Butternut Yellow (40)	Black (700)	Black (701)
Champagne (63)	Black (700)	Black (701)
Cortez Silver (69)	Black (700) Blue (703)	Black (701) Blue (704)
Dover White (50)	Black (700) Blue (703) Medium Green (708)	Black (701) Blue (704)
Dusk Blue (51)	Black (700) Blue (703)	Medium Green (707)
Fathom Green (57)	Black (700) Medium Green (708)	Black (701) Blue (704)
Frost Green (59)	Black (700) Medium Green (708)	Black (701) Medium Green (707)
Garnet Red (52)	Black (700)	Black (701) Medium Green (707)
Glacier Blue (53)	Black (700) Blue (703)	Black (701)
Lemans Blue (71)	Black (700)	Black (701) Blue (704)
Olympic Gold (65)	Black (700)	Black (701)
Tuxedo Black (10)	Black (700) Blue (703) Medium Green (703)	Black (701) Blue (704) Medium Green (707)

1969 TRIM CODES

<u>500 2 DR – 10137 BENCH SEATS</u>

BLACK (700) Black patterned thin vinyl leather
BLUE (703) Metallic dark blue thin vinyl leather
GREEN (708) Metallic medium green thin vinyl leather

<u>MONZA 2 DR AND CONVERTIBLE – 10537 & 10567 BUCKET SEATS</u>

BLACK (701) Black thin vinyl leather
BLUE (704) Metallic dark blue thin vinyl leather.
GREEN (707) Metallic medium green thin vinyl leather.

Chapter 7

Production Options

Regular Production Options

The following table is a list of regular production options offered and installed at the Chevrolet factories. There is a danger in compiling a list such as this as it is quite easy to leave options out. We researched this list carefully, but realize that our information may have been incomplete.

We did not attempt to list dealer installed options or aftermarket accessories or replications. There were a wide range of dealer supplied options including clocks, tissue boxes, multiplex speakers, luggage racks, and a host of items that were available for all General Motors cars, including the Corvair. Most of these were not specific to a year or model so were beyond the scope of this book. Below are photographs of some popular and not so popular options.

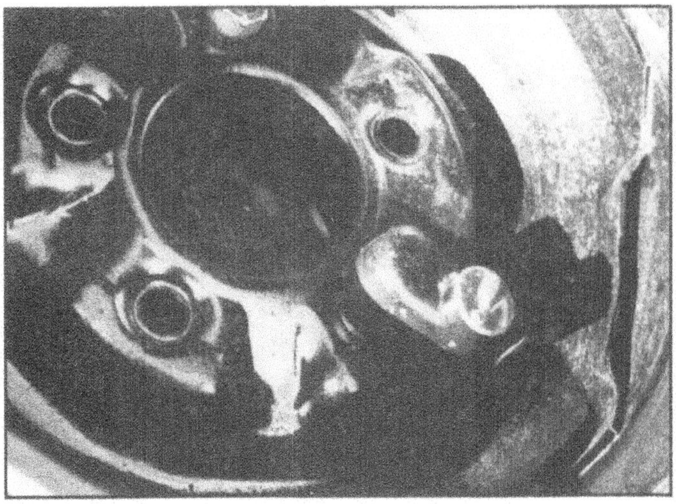

CORVAIR REGULAR PRODUCTION OPTIONS OFFERED 1960 THROUGH 1969

Option	500	700	Spyder	Monza	Corsa
BODY					
Air Conditioning	1961-1969	1961-1964	1964	1961-1969	1965-1966
Ash Tray Lamp	1967-1969	N.A.	N.A.	1967-1969	N.A.
Backup Lights	1960-1965 1966-Std.	1960-1964	Std.	Std. All Years	Std. All Years
Compass	1967 Only	N.A.	N.A.	1967 Only	N.A.
Day/Night Inside Mirror	1962-1966 1967-Std.	1962-1964	1964	1962-1966 1967- Std.	1965-1966
Door Edge Guards	1967-1969	N.A.	N.A.	1967-1969	N.A.
Electric Clock	1967-1969	N.A.	N.A.	1967-1969	N.A.
Emergency Road Kit	1967 Only	N.A.	N.A.	1967 Only	N.A.
Engine Compartment Lamp	1966-1969	N.A.	N.A.	1966-1969	1966
Fire Extinguisher w/ refill	1969	N.A.	N.A.	1969	N.A.
Floor Mat	1967-1969	N.A.	N.A.	1967-1969	N.A.
Fold Down Rear Seat	1960-1969	1960-1964	Std.	Std. All Years	Std. All Years
Front Armrests	1960-1961 1962-1969 Std.	1960-1961 1962-1964 Std	Std.	Std. All Years	Std. All Years
Front Seat Headrest, Conventional	1966-1968 1969 Std.	N.A.	N.A.	1966	1966
Front Seat Headrest, Contour	N.A.	N.A.	N.A.	1967-1968 1969 Std.	N.A.

CORVAIR REGULAR PRODUCTION OPTIONS OFFERED 1960 THROUGH 1969

Option	500	700	Spyder	Monza	Corsa
Glove Box Lamp	1965-1969	N.A.	N.A.	1965 1966-1969 Std.	1965 1966-1969 Std.
Heater and Defroster, Direct Air	1961 1962-1969 Std.	1961 1962-1964 Std.	Std. All Years	1961 1962-1969 Std.	Std. All Years
Heater and Defroster, Gasoline	1960-1962	1960-1962	N.A.	1960-1962	N.A.
Instrument Panel Courtesy Lights[2]	1967-1969	N.A.	N.A.	1967-1969	N.A.
Lighter	1960-1961 1962-1969 Std.	1960-1961 1962-1964 Std.	Std. All Years	Std. All Years	Std. All Years
Luggage Compartment Lamp	1966-1969	N.A.	N.A.	1966-1969	1966
Padded Dashboard	1960-1965 1966 Std.	1960-1964	1964	1960-1965 1966 Std.	1965-1966
Power Assist Folding Top (Convertibles)	N.A.	N.A.	1964	1962-1969	1965-1966
Radio, A.M. Manual	1960-1965	1960-1964	1964	1960-1965	1965-1966
Radio, A.M. Pushbutton	1961-1969	1961-1964	1964	1961-1969	1965-1966
Radio, A.M.-F.M. Pushbutton	1965-1969	N.A.	N.A.	1965-1969	1965-1966
Radio Antenna, Rear-Manual	1965-1969	N.A.	N.A.	1965-1969	1965-1966
Radio Antenna, Rear-Power	1966 Only	N.A.	N.A.	1966 Only	1966 Only
Radio Antenna, Fixed A.M.-F.M.	1967-1969	N.A.	N.A.	1967-1969	N.A.
Rear Door Armrests	1960-1961 1965-1966 1967 Std.	1960-1964	Std.	Std. All Years	Std. All Years

CORVAIR REGULAR PRODUCTION OPTIONS OFFERED 1960 THROUGH 1969

Option	500	700	Spyder	Monza	Corsa
Rear Seat Speaker (P.B. Radio Only)	1963-1969	1963-1964	1964	1963-1969	1965-1966
Rear View Mirror, Outside	1960-1965 1966 Std.	1960-1964	1964	1960-1965 1966 Std.	1965 1966 Std.
Rear View Mirror, Outside Remote Control	1964-1969	1964	1964	1964-1969	1965-1966
Rear Window Defroster	1968-1969	N.A.	N.A.	1968-1969	N.A.
Seat Belts, Front Only	1962-1967 1968 Std.	1962-1964	1964	1962-1967 1968 Std	1965-1966
Seat Belts, Custom Deluxe (With Retractors), Front	1964-1969	1964	1964	1964-1969	1965-1966
Seat Belt Shoulder Harness, Front	1966-1969	N.A.	N.A.	1966-1969	1966
Seat Belt Shoulder Harness, Front Custom Deluxe	1967-1969	N.A.	N.A.	1967-1969	N.A.
Seat Belts, Rear	1965-1967 1968 Std.	N.A.	N.A.	1965-1967 1968 Std.	1965-1966
Seat Belts, Custom Deluxe (With Retractors), Rear	1965-1969	N.A.	N.A.	1965-1969	1965-1966
Seat Belt Shoulder Harness, Rear	1968-1969	N.A.	N.A.	1968-1969	N.A.
Seat Belt Shoulder Harness, Rear Custom Deluxe	1968-1969	N.A.	N.A	1968-1969	N.A.
Spare Wheel Lock [3]	1961-1969	1961-1964	1964	1961-1969	1965-1966
Speed Warning Indicator	1967-1969	N.A.	N.A.	1967-1969	N.A.
Steering Wheel, Deluxe	1965-1969	N.A.	N.A.	1965-1969	1965-1966
Steering Wheel, Simulated Wood Grain	1964-1968	1964	1964	1964-1968	1965-1966
Stereo Tape Player	1967-1968	N.A.	N.A.	1967-1968	N.A.

CORVAIR REGULAR PRODUCTION OPTIONS OFFERED 1960 THROUGH 1969

Option	500	700	Spyder	Monza	Corsa
Sun Visor, Passenger Side	1960-1961 1962-1969 Std.	1960-1961 1962-1964 Std.	Std. 1964	Std. All Years	Std. All Years
Telescoping Steering Shaft	1965-1969	N.A.	N.A.	1965-1969	1965-1966
Tinted Glass, All Windows	1962-1969	1962-1964	1964	1962-1969	1965-1966
Tinted Windshield	1961-1969	1961-1964	1964	1961-1969	1965-1966
Traffic Hazard Warning Lights	1966 1967 Std.	N.A.	N.A.	1966 1967 Std	1966
Two Speed Windshield Wipers w/Washers	1962-1965 1966 Std.	1962-1964	1964	1962-1965 1966 Std.	1965 1966 Std.
Visor Vanity Mirror	1969	N.A.	N.A.	1969	N.A.
Wheel Covers, "Mag" Style	1966-1969	N.A.	N.A	1966-1969	1966
Wheel Covers [4]	1961-1969	1961-1964	1964.	1960-1969	1965-1966
Wheel Covers, Wire	1962-1969	1962-1964	1964	1962-1969	1965-1966
Wheel Trim Rings	1960-1961	1960-1961	N.A.	1960-1961	N.A.
Wheels, Wire [3]	1962-1964	1962-1964	1964	1962-1964	N.A.
Whitewall Tires 6.50 x 13 inches [3]	1960-1969	1960-1964	1964	1960-1969	1965-1966
Whitewall Tires 7.00 x 13 inches	N.A. 1966-1969	1961-1962 [3]	N.A.	1961-1962 [3] 1966-1969	1966
<u>CHASSIS</u>					
Bumper Guards, Front and Rear	1960-1969	1960-1964	1964	1960-1969	1965-1966
Heavy Duty 12 V Battery	1960-1961 1965-1969	1960-1961	N.A.	1960-1961 1965-1969	1965-1966

CORVAIR REGULAR PRODUCTION OPTIONS OFFERED 1960 THROUGH 1969

Option	500	700	Spyder	Monza	Corsa
Heavy Duty Suspension [3]	1962-1963 1965-1969	1962-1963	N.A.	1962-1963 1965-1969	1965-1966
Limited Slip Axle (Positraction)	1962-1969	1962-1969	1964	1962-1969	1965-1966
Metallic Brakes	1962-1963	1962-1963	N.A.	1962-1963	N.A.
Rear Axle (3.27:1)	1964-1966	1964	1964	1964-1966	1965-1966
Rear Axle (3.55:1)[3]	1961-1969	1961-1964	N.A.	1961-1969	N.A.
Rear Axle (3.89:1)	1960-1964	1960-1964	1964	N.A.	N.A.
Special Steering	1966-1969	N.A.	N.A.	1966-1969	1965-1966
Taxicab Equipment	1960-1961	1960-1961	N.A.	1960-1961	N.A.
<u>ENGINE</u> Air Cleaner, Pre Cleaner	1965-1966	N.A.	N.A.	1965-1966	Std.
Air Cleaner, Oil Bath	1964-1969	1964	1964	1964-1969	1965-1966
Air Injection Reactor[5]	1966-1967 1968 Std.	N.A.	N.A.	1966-1967 1968 Std.	1966
Crankcase Ventilation (P.C.V.)	1961-1962 1963 Std.	1961-1962 1963 Std.	1964	1961-1962 1963 Std.	1965-1966
Heavy Duty 47 Amp Alternator	1965-1967	N.A.	N.A.	1965-1967	1965-1966
Heavy Duty 35 Amp Generator	1960-1964	1960-1964	1964	1960-1964	N.A.
High Performance Engine (First Generation)	1960-1964	1960-1964	1964	1960-1964	N.A.
High Performance Engine 110 H.P.	1965-1969	N.A.	N.A.	1965-1969	1965-1966

CORVAIR REGULAR PRODUCTION OPTIONS OFFERED 1960 THROUGH 1969

Option	500	700	Spyder	Monza	Corsa
High Performance Engine 140 H.P.	1965-1969 except 1967	N.A.	N.A.	1965-1969 except 1967	Std.
Turbocharged Engine, First Generation	N.A.	N.A.	1964	1962-1963 Spyder Option	N.A.
Turbocharged Engine 180 H.P.	N.A.	N.A.	N.A.	N.A.	1965-1966
<u>TRANSMISSION</u>					
Automatic Transmission	1960-1969	1960-1964	N.A.	1960-1969	1965-1966
Four Speed Manual Transmission	1960-1969	1960-1964	Std.	1960-1969	1965-1966

1. Never offered on convertible models
2. Standard on all convertibles 1962 through 1969
3. All models except station wagons
4. Wheel cover design was distinctive for each model and changed most years (see text).
5. Mandatory in California beginning in 1966.

Index

W